IPHIGENIA IN FOREST HILLS

Also by Janet Malcolm

Burdock

Two Lives: Gertrude and Alice

Reading Chekhov: A Critical Journey

The Crime of Sheila McGough

The Silent Woman: Sylvia Plath and Ted Hughes

The Purloined Clinic: Selected Writings

The Journalist and the Murderer

In the Freud Archives

Psychoanalysis: The Impossible Profession

Diana and Nikon: Essays on Photography

Iphigenia in Forest Hills

Anatomy of a Murder Trial

JANET MALCOLM

Yale

UNIVERSITY PRESS

New Haven & London

Published with assistance from the Kingsley Trust Association Publication Fund
established by the Scroll and Key Society of Yale College.

A portion of this work was originally published in the *New Yorker*.

Yale University Press books may be purchased in quantity for educational,
business, or promotional use. For information, please e-mail sales.press@yale.edu
(U.S. office) or sales@yaleup.co.uk (U.K. office).

Designed by James J. Johnson and set in Sabon Roman type by
Keystone Typesetting, Inc.
Printed in the United States of America.

Library of Congress Cataloging-in-Publication Data

Malcolm, Janet.
Iphigenia in Forest Hills : anatomy of a murder trial / Janet Malcolm.
    p.   cm.
ISBN 978-0-300-16746-7 (cloth : alk. paper)

1. Borukhova, Mazoltuv — Trials, litigation, etc. 2. Mallayev, Mikhail — Trials,
litigation, etc. 3. Malakov, Daniel — Death and burial. 4. Trials (Murder) —
New York (State) — Queens County. 5. Murder for hire — New York (State) —
New York. 6. Jews, Bukharan — New York (State) — New York. 7. Queens
(New York, N.Y.) I. Title.
KF225.B67.M35   2011
345.747'24302523 — dc22
2010035851

A catalogue record for this book is available from the British Library.
This paper meets the requirements of ANSI/NISO Z39.48-1992
(Permanence of Paper).

10 9 8 7 6 5 4 3 2 1

To John Dunn

IPHIGENIA IN FOREST HILLS

And this is nothing different than any other murder case I've tried. You seem to think that this is so extraordinary. It's not. Somebody's life was taken, somebody's arrested, they're indicted, they're tried and they're convicted. That's all this is.

— Judge Robert Hanophy, April 21, 2009

Everything is ambiguous in life except in court.

— prospective juror (not selected) in voir dire,
January 29, 2009

I

AT around three in the afternoon on March 3, 2009, in the fifth week of the trial of Mazoltuv Borukhova — a thirty-five-year-old physician accused of murdering her husband — the judge turned to Borukhova's attorney, Stephen Scaring, and asked a pro forma question. "Do you have anything else, Mr. Scaring?" The trial was winding down. Two defense witnesses had just testified to Borukhova's good character, and Scaring was expected to rest his case with their modest, believable testimony. Scaring replied, without any special emphasis, "Yes, Your Honor. I think Dr. Borukhova will testify in her own defense."

There was no immediate reaction in the sparsely filled courtroom on the third floor of Queens Supreme Court, in Kew Gardens. Only after Borukhova had walked to the witness stand and taken the oath did the shock of Scaring's announcement register. The mouth of one of the spectators —that of the victim's younger brother—fell open, as if to mime the astonishment that ran through the room.

Borukhova had sat at the defense table throughout the trial and during the hearings that preceded it, writing on legal pads and occasionally looking up to whisper something in Scaring's ear or to exchange a charged glance with her mother and two sisters, who always sat in the second row of spectator seats. She was a small, thin woman of arresting appearance. Her features were delicate, and her skin had a gray pallor. At the hearings, she was dressed in a mannish black jacket and a floor-length black skirt, and she wore her long, dark, tightly curled hair hanging down her back, bound by a red cord. She looked rather like a nineteenth-century woman-student revolutionary. For the trial proper (perhaps on advice), she changed her appearance. She put her hair up and wore light-colored jackets and patterned long skirts. She looked pretty and charming, if undernourished. When she took the stand, she was wearing a white jacket.

Scaring, a tall, slender man of sixty-eight, is a criminal defense attorney of renown on Long Island. He has a reputation for taking cases that seem unwinnable — and winning them. But the Borukhova case had special difficulty. For one thing, Borukhova was not the only defendant; she was being tried together with Mikhail Mallayev, the man accused of killing her husband for her. Scaring wasn't defending him, however; a younger lawyer named Michael Siff was Mallayev's court-appointed counsel, and Siff did not have Scaring's capacity for performing impossible feats. Mallayev was likely to be convicted — there was strong forensic and eyewitness evidence against him — in which case Borukhova would have to be convicted, too, because of an unbreakable link to him: cell-phone records had established that in the three weeks preceding the murder there were ninety-one calls between her and Mallayev.

Another obstacle in the way of Scaring's game attempt to rescue Borukhova from a lifetime in prison was the lead prosecutor, Brad Leventhal, who does not have Scaring's experience — he is twenty years younger — but is an exceptionally formidable trial lawyer. He is a short, plump man with a mustache, who walks with the quick darting movements of a bantam cock and has a remarkably high voice, almost like a woman's, which at moments of excitement rises to the falsetto of a phonograph record played at the wrong speed. He uses his hands when he speaks, sometimes rubbing them in anticipation, sometimes throwing them up in gestures of helpless agitation. In his winter outerwear — a black calf-length coat and a black fedora — he could be taken for a Parisian businessman or a Bulgarian psychiatrist. In the courtroom, in his gray suit with an American flag pin in the lapel, and with his Queens-inflected speech, he plays the role of Assistant District Attorney for Queens (he is also the borough's chief of homicide) to the hilt. The second chair at the prosecution's table was filled by Donna Aldea, a handsome young assistant D.A. with an incandescent smile and a steely mind, who comes from the appellate division. Leventhal relied on her for producing unanswerable arguments before the judge on points of law.

2

I N his opening statement, Leventhal, standing directly in front of the jury and speaking without notes, set the scene of the murder — which occurred on October 28, 2007 — in the manner of an old-fashioned thriller:

It was a bright, sunny, clear, brisk fall morning, and on that brisk fall morning a young man, a young orthodontist by the name of Daniel Malakov, was walking down 64th Road in the Forest Hills section of Queens county just a few miles from where we are right now. With him was his little girl, his four-year-old daughter, Michelle.

Malakov, Leventhal continued, had left his office, full of waiting patients, to bring the child to a playground, a block away, for a day's visit with her mother, "his estranged wife," Mazoltuv Borukhova. Then, "as Daniel stood outside the entrance to Annadale playground, just feet from the entrance to that park, just feet from where his little girl stood, this defendant, Mikhail Mallayev, stepped out as if from nowhere. In his hand he had a loaded and operable pistol." When Leventhal uttered the words "this defendant," he theatrically extended his arm and pointed across the room to a thickset man in his fifties with a gray beard and heavy dark eyebrows, wearing wire-rimmed eyeglasses and a yarmulke, who sat impassively at the defense table. Leventhal went on to describe how Mallayev shot Malakov in the chest and in the back, and, as the orthodontist "lay on the ground dying, his blood pouring from his wounds, saturating his clothing and seeping onto the cement, this man, the defendant, who ended his life, calmly and coolly took his gun, put it into his jacket, turned away and headed up 64th Road towards 102nd Street, and fled the scene." With agitated outstretched hands Leventhal asked the jury:

Why? Why would this defendant lie in wait for an unsuspecting and innocent victim? A man, I will prove to you, he didn't even personally know. Why would he lie in wait with evil in his heart?

Leventhal answered the question:

Because he was hired to do it. He was paid to do it. He's an assassin. A paid assassin. An executioner. A hit man. For who? Who would hire this man, this defendant, to murder in cold blood an innocent victim in the presence of his own daughter? Who could have such strong feelings towards Daniel Malakov that they would hire an assassin to end his life? Who?

Leventhal walked toward the defense table and again lifted his arm and pointed—this time at Borukhova. "Her," Leventhal said, his voice rising to its highest pitch. "The defendant Mazoltuv Borukhova, Daniel Malakov's estranged wife. The woman with whom he had been engaged in an ongoing and heated, contentious, acrimonious divorce for years."

Leventhal spoke for another fifty minutes, the spell of his storytelling occasionally broken by objections from the opposing attorneys but always restored by the power of his narration. Most of these objections were overruled by the judge, who repeatedly told the jury, "What they say in their opening statement is not evidence."

What they say in their opening statements is decisive, of course. If we understand that a trial is a contest between competing narratives, we can see the importance of the first appearance of the narrators. The impression they make on the jury is indelible. An attorney who bores and irritates the jury during his opening statement, no matter what evidence he may later produce, has put his case at fatal risk.

Leventhal was followed by Siff, who bored and irritated the jury to the point that a young juror raised his hand and asked to go to the bathroom. Siff, guilelessly, began by complimenting Leventhal on his performance: "Excellent presentation by the lawyer. Excellent advocate for the county." And: "Mr. Leventhal did an awesome job. I'm sitting here now looking at my notes and I was amazed how he could just reel off all that stuff without a paper." He went on to give a floundering, meandering speech about the "presumption of innocence" in which "my client is cloaked" that only underscored the likelihood of Mallayev's guilt. Siff's second chair was filled by Michael Anastasiou, an affable defense lawyer who has a pleasing courtroom manner but who participated minimally in the proceedings.

Scaring's culminating bad break was to draw Robert Hanophy as his trial judge. Not many acquittals have occurred in Hanophy's court. In a 2005 article, a *Daily News* reporter named Bob Port wrote that Hanophy is known as Hang 'em Hanophy and "is widely believed to have imprisoned more murderers than any sitting judge in the United States." "I don't have anything else but homicides," Hanophy told Port. "That's all I try. I like what I do. I love it." Scaring had asked Hanophy to recuse himself on the ground that his son and his daughter worked in the D.A.'s office, which would bias him in favor of the prosecution. He also asked for a separate trial for Borukhova. The hanging judge turned down both requests.

Hanophy is a man of seventy-four with a small head and a large body and the faux-genial manner that American petty tyrants cultivate. From his dais he looks out over the courtroom, taking in every spectator as well as every actor in the drama being played out under his direction. "You there with the cap," he will raise his voice to say to a spectator. "Take it off. You can't wear that in here." In 1997, Hanophy was censured by the New York State Commission on Judicial Conduct for making "undignified, discourteous and disparaging remarks" and being "mean-spirited" and "vituperative" during a sentencing. The remarks were directed not at the defendant — a pathetic young Englishwoman named Caroline Beale, who, eighteen months earlier, had killed the baby she had given birth to alone in a Manhattan hotel room — but at the British nation.

Beale was obviously insane when she stuffed the newborn into a plastic bag and then attempted to take the corpse out of the country hidden under her clothes. But after she was arrested at the airport, she wasn't sent to a mental hospital. She was charged with murder and imprisoned at Rikers Island for eight months. The intervention of an Irish-American lawyer named Michael Dowd finally ended the mad girl's ordeal. Dowd negotiated a plea bargain whereby she would admit her guilt and receive a sentence of five years' probation, eight months of prison time (already served), and a year of psychiatric treatment. Three days before the sentencing, Beale's parents expressed outrage at the treatment their mentally ill daughter had received in this country, calling the American system of justice "medieval." Their remarks were widely reported in the press. At the sentencing, Hanophy lashed back—and sort of went mad himself. He read a statement in which he characterized British law as "primitive and uncivilized" because it "grants a blanket exemption from prosecution or punishment to those people who kill their children, when their children are under the age of one." He went on to characterize England as "that great country that has convicted a great many people on the perjured testimony of their police, allowed them to spend fifteen or seventeen years in prison. Did everything to see that they remained in prison, even though they knew, or should have known, they didn't belong there." This remarkable statement—which had nothing to do with the Beale case, and came out of Hanophy's viewing of the film *In the Name of the Father,* about the unjust conviction of three Irishmen and one Englishwoman for a terrorist bombing—is a measure of what judges feel they can permit themselves in their courtrooms. The absolute power they enjoy eats away at the self-doubt that the rest of us depend on to keep ourselves more or less in line. Hanophy went too far over the line (on top of everything else, he couldn't resist calling Beale's father "the guy with the big mouth"), and he had his knuckles rapped by the Commission on Judicial Conduct. But there is no reason to think that the commissioners' harsh words have had any effect on Hanophy's courtroom style. A document of censure has no consequences. Hanophy's power remains un-changed, and he continues to exercise it with evident enjoy-ment, and without any sign of doubt.

3

SCARING'S courtroom manner is low-key and courtly and touched with a certain hauteur. He wears the cus-tomary lawyer's pinstriped suit, but when he gets up to examine a witness, he does not rebutton the jacket the way lawyers on television do (and the way Siff does). Scaring moves with elegant ease and speaks in a soft, benign voice — until, during a cross-examination, he makes the obligatory accusatory turn. Then he permits his voice to rise and his tone to take on a nasty edge. He has a little gray in his black hair, and his swarthy face sometimes looks haggard. He has a sweet smile. His hearing isn't good.

Scaring began his kindly, almost tender, examination of Borukhova with a series of biographical inquiries. Her an-swers established that she had been born in Uzbekistan, in the former Soviet Union, and had lived in the city of Sa-markand, where she went to high school and then to medi-cal school, from which she received a degree in general medicine and surgery at the age of twenty-two. Scaring did not ask Borukhova about her religion. Trial lawyers are storytellers who try to keep the lines of their stories straight and clean. The story of the Bukharan Jewish sect, to which the defendants and victim and their respective families belonged, is a maddeningly complex and untidy one.

The untidiness begins with the name. "Bukharan" refers both to the ancient city of Bukhara and to the emirate of Bukhara that intermittently ruled over a large region in Central Asia between the sixteenth and the twentieth centuries. The term "Bukharan Jews" is said to have been coined by European travelers to the emirate in the sixteenth century. No one really knows how or why or when these mysterious Jews came to Central Asia. Legend has it that they are descendants of one of the lost tribes of Israel who never returned from Babylonian captivity in the sixth century B.C. Histories of the sect are tangled accounts of stubborn survival over two thousand years under Persian, Mongol, Arab, Imperial Russian, and, finally, Soviet Russian rule. Like the Jews of Eastern Europe and Spain, the Bukharan Jews were kept out of agriculture and nudged into commerce and craft, at which they excelled. The language, Bukhori, developed as a dialect of the Tajik-Farsi language into a mixture of Farsi, Hebrew, and Russian. In the 1970s large numbers of Bukharan Jews immigrated to Israel and the United States, and after the breakup of the Soviet Union almost all the Bukharan Jews remaining in Central Asia left for these countries. Today, there are a hundred thousand Bukharan Jews in Israel and sixty thousand in the United States—most of them living in the Forest Hills–Rego Park section of Queens.

Under Scaring's examination, Borukhova related—in accented and slightly imperfect English—that she had come to the United States in 1997, studied English for a year, and then taken her medical boards; this was followed by a three-year residency at a hospital in Brooklyn. In 2005 she became licensed to practice, and in 2006 she became board-certified. Scaring then turned to Borukhova's marriage to Daniel Malakov, in 2002. "How did you get along with your in-laws?" he asked.

"There was a problem to begin with," she replied.

"What was the problem?"

"They never wanted us to get married."

Earlier, her father-in-law, Khaika Malakov, had testified for the prosecution. He is a tall, vividly handsome man in his late sixties who has something of the louche emotionality of a character in an Isaac Bashevis Singer story. Scaring, attempting in his opening statement to discredit the Malakov family's accusations against Borukhova on the day of the murder, said, "Daniel's father is an actor in the community. You know what actors do — they make things up." This is absurd, of course: actors merely speak their lines; they don't invent them. It was Scaring who was making things up. If any profession (apart from the novelist's) is in the business of making things up, it is the profession of the trial lawyer. The "evidence" in trials is the thread out of which lawyers spin their tales of guilt or innocence. With his examination of Borukhova, Scaring was offering an alternative to the story that Leventhal had told in his opening and then retold through the testimony of his witnesses. He would take the same evidence that, in Leventhal's tale, demonstrated Borukhova's guilt, and use it to demonstrate her innocence.

The fourth week of the trial had produced an arresting

illustration of the malleability of trial evidence. During a police search of Borukhova's apartment, an audiotape had been found and seized. It was a garbled, fragmentary, almost inaudible recording, on a mini-cassette, of a conversation between Borukhova and Mallayev, speaking in Bukhori and Russian. The conversation had taken place in May, 2007 — five months before the murder. The prosecution had asked an F.B.I. translator named Mansur Alyadinov to make an English translation and called him to the courtroom to read from his text as the tape was played. The conversation had been recorded by Borukhova during a ride in a car — secretly, Alyadinov deduced, when he heard the sound of cloth being rubbed, meaning that the microphone had been hidden under clothes. But what was being discussed was not a murder plot. The tape recorded one of those irritatingly banal conversations that we helplessly overhear on trains and in restaurants from people talking on cell phones. The fragments of boring dialogue that came through had no relevance to the case. Why, then, was Leventhal playing the tape to the jury? The reason became apparent in the final two lines. The courtroom suddenly awakened from its torpor as it heard Mallayev say to Borukhova, "Are you going to make me happy?" And Borukhova replied, "Yes."

One can imagine the translator's own happiness when he heard these lines — and Leventhal's when he read them in the transcript. Two interpretations immediately present themselves — both damning. The first is that Mallayev was sleeping with Borukhova and asking about a future encounter. The second is that Mallayev was talking about money — was she going to make him happy by giving him money to murder her husband? In either case, it looked bad for Borukhova. However, when Scaring cross-examined Alyadinov, it began to look less bad. This is the idea and beauty of the cross-examination. A successful cross-examination is like a turn of the roulette wheel that restores a lost fortune. First, citing a translation that Borukhova had made for him, Scaring got the F.B.I. translator to concede that, among other blunders, he had omitted the English words "Mother's Day" from his text and that a mystifying discussion of a "crazy house" was actually a discussion of the madhouse that the airport was on the day — Mother's Day — that Mallayev traveled to New York from his home, in Chamblee, Georgia. Then Scaring took care of "Are you going to make me happy?" In Borukhova's translation, what Mallayev had said was "Are you getting off?" The car had reached its destination. He had used the word *padayesh* — literally meaning "Are you falling?" — in an idiomatic sense to ask if she was getting out of the car. The translator had heard *padayesh* as *obraduesh* ("Are you going to make me happy?"). The mistake was understandable: on a very hard-to-hear tape the word could easily be misheard. But that the mishearing so favored the prosecution, that it so well advanced the narrative of an unsavory association, suggests that this was a mishearing by design — unconscious, perhaps, but design nonetheless. We go through life mishearing and mis-seeing and misunderstanding so that the stories we tell ourselves will add up. Trial lawyers push this human tendency to a higher level. They are playing for higher stakes than we are playing for when we tinker with actuality in order to transform the tale told by an idiot into an orderly, self-serving narrative.

4

A WEEK before Scaring startled the courtroom by calling Borukhova to the witness stand, he stopped a journalist named William Gorta in the hallway outside the courtroom and said, "What do you think? Should I put her on the stand?"

Gorta replied, "God no!" Scaring looked at him questioningly and Gorta said, "If you put her on the stand, Leventhal will kill her." Gorta, a former New York City cop who now covers the Queens courts for the *New York Post*, was one of five journalists who came regularly to the trial and sat in the first row of spectator seats, which bear a sign saying "Attorneys only" but where the press may also sit. The four other journalists were Nicole Bode, of the *Daily News*; Anne Bernard, of the *New York Times*; Ivan Pereira, of the *Forest Hills Ledger*; and me, representing the *New Yorker*. Hanophy was aware of us—as he was aware of everyone and everything going on in the courtroom, his fiefdom. The other spectator seats were occupied largely by members of the families of the defendants and the victim, who sat on opposite sides of the aisle, as if this were a wedding with a bride's side and a groom's side. The groom's side — behind the prosecution's table and the jury box — was always well filled. Khaika Malakov never missed a day, and came surrounded by a horde of relatives and friends — mostly men — whose atmosphere of anger and aggression made one want to run from them, as if from a disturbed swarm of hornets. During recesses, this horde would move into the hallway and cluster around Leventhal and, on the days of their testimony, Leventhal's police witnesses.

The bride's side was more sparsely filled. The regulars were Borukhova's mother, Istat, and her sisters Sofya and Natella, who came with prayer books, from which they read to themselves. Where the Malakov family liked to talk to the daily press, and were often quoted in it, the Borukhova family refused all overtures from journalists. They sat barricaded by a wall of reticence and an aura of arrogance and disdain. They were sometimes joined by Borukhova's brother, Shlomo, and, occasionally, by a young boy. The sisters wore floor-length skirts and wigs of bouffant curly hair. The mother, thin and worn, did not take off a long belted brown overcoat and felt hat. During the year of hearings that preceded the trial, there were incidents of insults hurled across the aisle, but, by the time of the trial proper, the families had been subdued into surly silence by Hanophy's threats of eviction from the courtroom. A lone young woman sat behind the Borukhova mother and sisters: Mallayev's daughter, Maya.

Scaring asked his careful, kind questions, and Borukhova told of her separation from Daniel Malakov some months after the birth of Michelle, in 2003, followed by two attempts at reconciliation, and by a final separation in April, 2005. He asked her about her "custody dispute" with Daniel and about the "transfer of custody" that had taken place six days before the murder.

The dispute over the child had given Leventhal his motive for the crime. On October 3rd, three and a half weeks before the murder, a State Supreme Court judge named Sidney Strauss issued a decision that — in Leventhal's words — "unknowingly and unwittingly would result in Daniel's murder." Strauss ruled that four-year-old Michelle — who had lived all her life with her mother — must now go and live with her father. A stunned Borukhova appealed the decision, and was turned down; nineteen days later, the "transfer" of a hysterically screaming child from the arms of her mother to those of her father took place. "If Daniel's fate had not been sealed when Judge Strauss issued that ruling, on October 3 of 2007, it was most certainly sealed on the evening of October 22 of 2007," Leventhal said in his opening. His narrative now had its mythic underpinning. It was as inevitable that Borukhova — "her" — would revenge herself on Daniel for the loss of Michelle as that Clytemnestra would revenge herself on Agamemnon for the loss of Iphigenia.

By putting Borukhova on the stand, Scaring hoped to dismantle that story. He would convince the jury that the young physician who answered his questions with such modesty and sincerity could not possibly be a murderer.

Yes, there was evidence against her — the ninety-one cell-phone calls could not be gotten around — but everything one knew about life and about people cried out against the notion that this gentle, cultivated woman was the mastermind of a criminal plot. Through his examination Scaring proposed to transform Leventhal's archetypal avenging murderess into an ordinary beleaguered working mom. The phone calls would be explained. The "rush to judgment" by the police would be exposed for the mistake it was.

Under Scaring's questioning, Borukhova outlined her arduous schedule as a hospitalist at two hospitals, Westchester Square and White Plains, where she worked twenty-four-hour shifts, and as an attending physician at Forest Hills North Shore. She related that at eight o'clock on the night before the murder, she began her twenty-four-hour shift at White Plains, which, however, because of a special circumstance, she had arranged to end after twelve hours. The special circumstance was a visit with Michelle that Malakov had granted her. After she returned from her night at the hospital, she would meet him at the Annadale playground and he would deliver Michelle to her for an all-day visit. A plan for activities with cousins — the children of Borukhova's sisters Ludmila and Sofya — was in place. But no time had been set for the meeting in the playground. "My husband wasn't the person who would limit himself into the time," Borukhova said, and cited the four or five cell-phone calls between herself and Malakov that were made in the hour before the meeting in the playground, culminating in a call in which he says, "Marina, I see you," as he walks toward her on the street. (Marina was the name family members used, rather than Mazoltuv.)

When Borukhova reached this point in her narrative, she broke down. "Take your time, Marina," Scaring said.

"I'm so sorry," Borukhova said. She composed herself and went on, "I kneeled and I opened my arms and Michelle start running." She went on:

> I picked her up and I swinged. I did like two swings or maybe three and by the time I was finished we all were laughing. We all were so happy and Daniel also. He was — he was very happy with his — with his — I don't know — bright smile. And he approached and now he was holding her buttocks and legs and I was holding her upper body and the arms and neck and we were together now swinging her. . . . And we were swinging and Michelle likes the wind. We were blowing the wind like "whoo" to her face and we all were happy and we were laughing.

Scaring asked, "What were you saying, if anything, while you were doing that?"

Borukhova said, "We were not saying anything, we were just laughing and we all were happy."

"And then something happened?"

"After a long time I felt like a family again. And we were swinging and she was very happy. We were happy. We were all laughing. And all of the sudden I felt heavy. I felt I can't hold her." Malakov had dropped Michelle's legs and buttocks, said a few words in Russian (when Borukhova began to quote him, Leventhal objected and was sustained), and run into the street. "He's looking at me and I look at him. His face is pale and I see his face is like torturing, like twitched in pain. I was looking at him and he's holding his chest. . . . I see the blood."

What is most remarkable about Borukhova's account of the shooting of her husband is its soundlessness. Her first awareness that something was wrong was not the sound of gunfire, but the unsupported weight of the child. Her account is like a silent film. It immediately aroused the suspicion of the police. When a detective "asked me if I heard something or if I see somebody running, I said I didn't hear anything, I didn't see anybody. And he said people heard the shots three blocks away and you were right there and you didn't hear. You have to come up with a better story." Borukhova never changed her strange story. She always insisted that she never heard the shots.

On the stand, Borukhova continued her account: "I don't remember all my actions, but I remember taking Michelle and running, but when I was running I was still looking at him." She saw Malakov fall to the ground. She found herself on a bench in the playground, near the swings, where she held the child in her arms. "I was screaming and crying but I remember my daughter, she hold my hand like this and she said, 'Mommy, don't cry.' " Borukhova left the child in the playground with a woman she knew and ran back to the street to try to revive the man whose life was ebbing from him. She did chest compressions and mouth-to-mouth resuscitation. When a police officer arrived, she asked for emergency medical equipment—an ambu bag and equipment for intubation—which he didn't have. He helped her with chest compressions. When a police emergency medical squad arrived, the medical workers pushed her away. They had the proper medical equipment but used it clumsily. She watched helplessly as they struggled and failed to intubate Malakov. "Let me do it, let me do it. I do it on a daily basis," she said to them. Finally they allowed her to perform the intubation. But Malakov did not respond, and was put on a stretcher and taken in an ambulance to the nearby North Shore Hospital, where he died. Borukhova began to feel chest pain and nausea, and was taken to North Shore in another ambulance. She thought she was having a heart attack. Some of her in-laws were already at the hospital. They were "screaming and blaming me." Her sister-in-law Nalia "was accusing me. 'You killed him, you killed him, you killed him.'" Borukhova was taken to another room, where a detective named Ismet Hoxha interviewed her.

"He accused you of killing your husband?" Scaring said.

"Yes, he did."

"What did he say?"

Borukhova answered that Hoxha said, "They found the guy who killed my husband," and that "I should help myself." She added, "He promised me that if I cooperate that he's gonna talk to the D.A. and he's gonna give me good deal."

Hoxha was lying. The guy who killed the orthodontist and coolly put the gun in his pocket had not yet been found. He had disappeared — though not quite without a trace. He had left behind a silencer made out of a bleach bottle, which had been taped to the gun and had fallen off, dislodged by the first shot. The police matched fingerprints on the tape with fingerprints of Mikhail Mallayev that had been on file with the New York City police since 1994, when he was arrested at a Manhattan subway station for fare-beating. But the fingerprint match only confirmed what the police already had on Mallayev: the record of his cellphone calls with Borukhova. Through them, he was traced to his house in Chamblee; he was arrested there and extradited to Queens. To clinch the matter, an eyewitness to the shooting identified him in a lineup. But it was months before these triumphs of police detection would occur.

When I wrote that Hoxha was lying when he said that the killer had been found, I did so on the assumption that Borukhova was telling the truth when she quoted him to that effect. Of course, this is an assumption I should not have made. Hoxha may never have uttered those words — Borukhova may have invented them. If witnesses abided by the oath to "tell the truth, the whole truth, and nothing but the truth," there wouldn't be the contradictions between testimonies that give a trial its tense plot and the jury its task of deciding whom to believe. In his cross-examination of Hoxha, who testified at length for the prosecution, Scaring said harshly, "At the hospital, you accused her of killing her husband, didn't you?" and Hoxha said, "No." Scaring went on, "You said 'If you admit you killed your husband it will go easy for you,' didn't you?" and Hoxha again made a denial. Whom to believe, Hoxha or Borukhova? *Padayesh* or *obraduesh*?

5

DURING the voir dire, to illustrate the problematic of bias, Scaring held up an example from baseball: the close call. "Let's say that you're rooting for the Yankees or you're rooting for the Mets and they're playing in the World Series," he said. "It's the ninth inning and it looks like it could be a home run, but it hits very close to the foul/fair line. You might see it as fair or you might see it as foul — not because you want to lie but because *it's what you want*." Jurors are not supposed to want anything. They are supposed to follow the match of the opposing attorneys in a state of dumb desirelessness. No rooting in the courtroom, please. But rooting is in our blood; we take sides as we take breaths. The voir dire is nothing if not a recognition of the unattainability of the ideal of neutrality and the inescapability of bias. It's a guessing game — each attorney, as he questions a prospective juror, tries to sniff out his inclinations. A juror who wants to be picked knows better than to reveal them. He has been admonished by the judge to be "open-minded" and "fair" and "objective," and he keeps his mouth shut lest he betray that he is none of those things. In the Mallayev-Borukhova voir dire, the jurors who were picked were the most laconic ones — the ones who said almost nothing. The first juror chosen — who thus became the jury foreman — was a young man named Christopher Fleming, who had just graduated from Siena College as a major in finance. His answers to the judge's, Leventhal's, Scaring's, and Siff's questions were exemplary. He was like a discreet secretary to a politician, veiled but polite, reserved but respectful. Each side accepted him without demurral, and each evidently had high hopes for his predisposition toward itself.

Each side receives a certain number of peremptory challenges, whereby it can dismiss prospective jurors without giving a reason. There are also challenges for cause. Here reasons for dismissal are given: the prospective juror said that he couldn't be neutral after reading about the case in the newspapers, or he replied yes to the question "Do you think police officers are more believable than ordinary citizens?" If the judge grants the challenge for cause, the challenging attorney does not use up one of his peremptory challenges. In 1986 the peremptory challenge was itself challenged, in a case called *Batson v. Kentucky*. In the voir dire for the trial of a black man named James Kirkland Batson, accused of burglary, the prosecutor had used his peremptory strikes to dismiss four black prospective jurors; an all-white jury was seated and the defendant was convicted. The case came before the Supreme Court, which ruled that the peremptory challenge could not be used if the reason not given was manifestly a reason of race. In subsequent decisions, the ruling was extended to gender, ethnicity, and religion.

In the Mallayev-Borukhova voir dire, the Batson decision was invoked three times by Scaring and twice by Leventhal. Scaring's first two attempts to persuade the judge that the prosecution was "trying to knock out as many women as they possibly can" were rebuffed, but his third succeeded. Hanophy conceded that Leventhal's peremptory strike against a young woman named Laurie Rosen did reveal a pattern of discrimination against women, and Rosen was seated as a juror, to Leventhal's fury and Scaring's satisfaction — which, however, was short-lived. Rosen, who worked as a physical therapist with disabled children (and had replied, when asked to name her hobbies, "sports, cooking, and autism awareness"), came back after lunch and tearfully begged to be let off; she hadn't realized what sequestration would mean for her night work with autistic children. Leventhal and Scaring locked horns again, and now Hanophy sided with Leventhal and let Rosen go. "This is a voir dire out of hell," the court clerk was heard saying to a court officer.

It was the fifth day of jury selection and several places in the jury box remained unfilled. Hundreds of potential jurors had entered the courtroom, and the majority of them had exited it after Hanophy announced that this was a five-week trial with possible sequestration at the end and asked if this would be a hardship for anyone. It was a hardship for almost everyone, and Hanophy was lenient with all but a few supplicants. Among those whose excuses were found wanting was a young high school teacher who was preparing students for an advanced placement examination in European history and economics and felt that his presence at the school was urgently needed. His direct plea to the judge failing, the teacher resorted to the subterfuge of answering the attorneys' questions with such flagrant intelligence and subtlety that there was no chance of his being selected. Leventhal challenged him for cause and neither Scaring nor Siff objected.

After losing Rosen, Scaring had to endure the torment of seeing a man named Stein seated on the jury. When Scaring used his last peremptory against Stein, Leventhal riposted with a Batson challenge — he said Scaring was systematically knocking off men. Scaring fought ferociously to keep Stein off the jury. He argued that he had challenged Stein — a stout, older white man from Floral Park who worked for the New York City Department of Transportation — not because he was a male but because he was "Mr. Prosecution Juror." Look at him: "His hair is cropped just perfect, mustache, comes from a conservative town, works for the City of New York." Scaring pointed to other white male jurors (such as Fleming) he had not challenged. But the judge upheld Leventhal, and Stein was seated as the second alternate juror. The next morning, at sidebar, Scaring made a last desperate stand against Stein. He said he had spoken with a jury consulting firm to advise me as to what some of the issues might be concerning jury selection given the fact that my client is a Russian immigrant, Jewish Russian immigrant, that my client dresses differently than most. Her clothes, her dress. Long dresses which go right down to her feet. She has her hair which she's got in a bun now but it's very long. Her sisters who likely will testify wear wigs because they're married, and they're pretty ugly wigs. I mean, they stand out. They also wear the long dresses. So this is a unique Jewish community from Russia. My consulting firm said that I should be very cautious of Germans.

During the long colloquy between Scaring and Hanophy that followed (with sparring about whether the fact that Floral Park had a large German population and a famous German restaurant named Koenig's proved that Stein was German), the unsaid got said. "We make judgments based upon people's appearances," Scaring said. And "the reason a defendant has an experienced lawyer is because an experienced lawyer has insight with regard to the kind of jurors that will be more favorable to her than to the prosecution or more favorable to the prosecution." A few days earlier, Leventhal, referring to Borukhova, had asked a panel of prospective jurors, "Does anybody here feel that because she holds a medical degree, because she's an educated woman, because she went and advanced herself in education, does anybody here feel that that's going to impact upon your ability to evaluate the evidence in this case?" There was no response. If I had been on that panel, I would, in all honesty, have had to raise my hand. But if I had concealed my sisterly bias Leventhal — after looking at me and hearing me speak — would nevertheless have recognized me as Ms. Defense Juror and kicked me off the jury panel as fast as he could.

6

My fellow journalists were made of sterner stuff. Ivan Pereira, a very young man, of slight build and terse speech, was a fervid rooter for the home team. He had been one of the first journalists at the crime scene, and had reported on the case in the *Ledger* for the next twenty-two months. He had an understandably proprietary feeling about the murder. He had watched the police build their case, and there was no doubt in his mind of the defendants' guilt and despicableness. Gorta, a bearded man in his fifties, who plays the role of the hard-bitten journalist whom nothing can surprise, and who is extremely kind, was a more circumspect prosecution fan. During the proceedings, he chewed gum and, when he wasn't taking notes, worked on crossword puzzles. Nicole Bode, a willowy, blond, very pretty, and also very kind woman in her late twenties, read *Granta* when she wasn't taking notes, and also quietly favored the prosecution. She and Gorta filed pithy daily stories for their respective tabloids under raffish headlines ("HE DRILLS DENTIST: SLAY CASE"). The courthouse was their beat and sometimes they would have to dash off to a newsworthy trial on another floor.

Anne Barnard, a handsome young brunette, was the queen of the reporters' cohort. While Gorta's and Bode's stories had to take their modest place among the axe-murder and sex-scandal stories of the *News* and the *Post,* and Pereira's among the rezoning reports of the *Ledger,* Barnard's articles had little if any competition in the *Times;* hers was almost invariably the only murder-trial story of the day. Most enviably, Barnard was given the space that the others frustratingly lacked for conveying a sense of the small movements by which the trial was propelled. The *Times* had started to cover the case a year before Barnard's assignment to it; the Bukharan Jewish connection evidently distinguished it from the ordinary sordid murder that the *Times* leaves to the tabloids. "Doctor Is Charged in a Killing, and Her People Bear the Shame" was the headline of a *Times* story of February 17, 2008. The reporter, Cara Buckley, had gone into the Bukharan Jewish community and interviewed people on the street along with relatives of the victim and the defendant. ("Why this happened, I cannot say. Now the Bukharans are in shame, for the first time ever.") Barnard, who speaks Russian, continued to mine the Bukharan vein in her initial story of February 9, 2009 ("As One of Their Own Is Tried for Murder, Bukharans Debate Loss of Old Ways"), but, as the trial wore on, her attention began to shift from the yentas on 108th Street in Forest Hills to the characters in the courtroom. Whether to reflect the grandness of the *Times* or in accordance with a personal code, Barnard dressed differently from the rest of us. She wore interesting, beautiful dresses and skirts in contrast to the uninteresting jeans and corduroys and sweaters that Gorta and Bode and Pereira and I wore. Her sharp-eyed stories about the trial were as pleasing as her elegant clothes; not the least of the pleasure we took in them was the knowledge that Judge Hanophy would be irked by them.

Journalists are thought to be competitive, and sometimes they are, but their main feeling about one another is fraternal. Journalists love one another the way members of a family—in their case, a kind of crime family—do. In *Democracy in America,* Alexis de Tocqueville wrote of American journalists as persons of "low social status, [whose] education is only sketchy, and [whose] thoughts are often vulgarly expressed." He went on to note that "the hallmark of the American journalist is a direct and coarse attack, without any subtleties, on the passions of his readers; he disregards principles to seize on people, following them into their private lives and laying bare their weaknesses and their vices." Over the years, the social status and the education level of journalists has risen, and some journalists write extremely well. But the profession retains its transgressiveness. Human frailty continues to be the currency in which it trades. Malice remains its animating impulse. A trial offers unique opportunities for journalistic heartlessness. When the malignant, often libelous words of battling attorneys are lifted out of the heated context of the trial and set in cold type, a new, more exquisite torture is suffered by the object of their abuse — who now stands exposed to the world's abuse. Journalists attending a long trial together develop a special camaraderie born of a shared good mood: their stories are writing themselves; they have only to pluck the low-hanging fruit of the attorneys' dire narratives. They can sit back and enjoy the show.

At the genial invitation of Gorta and Bode, I sometimes joined them for lunch in the press office on the first floor of the courthouse, from which they filed their stories, a place of appealing scruffiness — it could have been a set for a 1930s comedy about newspaper reporters — furnished with beat-up unmatched office furniture and rusted metal file cabinets and strewn with newspapers and paper cups and the debris of years of transient occupation. Bode and Gorta would eat side by side at a pair of anachronistic computers, chatting as they typed, and I would clear a space for my sandwich at an unused desk covered with yellowed copies of the *Post* and the *News*. When they weren't at their offices outside the courthouse, Barnard and Pereira also congregated here.

As time went on, though, when lunchtime came I found myself gravitating toward a bench in a corridor off the courthouse lobby, where I awaited a woman named Alla Lupyan-Grafman. She was a Russian-speaker who sat at the defense table throughout the trial as a court-appointed interpreter for the defendants. Both defendants spoke English — Borukhova in particular had no need of an interpreter — but the court had made the appointment to be on the safe side, to ensure that no issue of language interfered with the smooth whirring of the wheels of justice. Alla was a slender, stylishly dressed, exceptionally friendly woman in her late forties, with a mane of curly platinum-blond hair, with whom, by the end of the trial, every lawyer, court officer, journalist, and even some spectators were on ecstatic hugging terms. She, too, was an immigrant from the former Soviet Union, but not a Bukharan; she was an Ashkenazi Jew from Minsk.

Over lunch, Alla spoke of the xenophobia of the earlier Russian-Jewish immigrants toward the newcomers from Central Asia and cited some of the more extravagantly stereotypic characterizations: the Bukharans were alien and not altogether civilized — savage, tribal people, capable of violence, even of murder. They were Jews but not proper Jews, more like Muslims than like Jews. They had dirty living habits — things were strewn about in their front yards. On the other hand, some of them were mysteriously, sinisterly rich, and built showy McMansions that had no place in haimish Forest Hills.

Alla had a special complaint about the Bukharans — a linguistic one. She said that the older generation had never learned proper Russian, even though it was an official language under the Soviets. When Khaika Malakov testified — with an interpreter simultaneously translating — she was highly critical of his Russian. She was uncritical of Borukhova's Russian — and she was sympathetic to Borukhova herself. She and I offered each other tastes of the sandwiches and fruit we had brought from home, and struggled with the enigma of the case: she couldn't have done it and she must have done it.

7

COURTROOMS are temples of waiting. Those of us who came daily to the theater of the Mallayev-Borukhova trial learned that the curtain time of 9:30 A.M. meant nothing and preceded a wait of at least an hour. The entire cast of characters — the attorneys, the defendants, the witnesses, the court stenographer, the interpreter, and the judge — never contrived to assemble at the designated hour. Only the house factotums — the courtroom clerk, the judge's clerk, and five or six armed officers — came on time and calmly occupied the stage; the clerks fussed with papers on their desks and took telephone calls, and the police officers lounged against walls, drinking bottled water and kidding one another. The spectators who had not yet learned to gauge how late they could be without forfeiting a desirable seat, and who regretted their punctuality, watched them closely for signs of heightened alertness.

An attorney was sometimes the cause of the delay, but more often than not it was the late arrival of one or both of the defendants, who were being held in separate prisons on Rikers Island and were driven to the courthouse in separate vans. When news of the defendants' arrival would somehow be communicated—I never was quick enough to see how—the focus of the spectators' attention became a locked wooden door at the left of the defense table. Officers and attorneys went in and out of it—to an elaborate ritual of unlocking and locking. Finally, after the attorneys came through the door for the last time and took their places at the defense table, and the judge mounted his dais, the defendants arrived in the courtroom. There was always something shocking about this entrance. I never got used to it. The wooden door would suddenly open and Mallayev and Borukhova, handcuffed behind their backs, and flanked by armed officers, who held them by the arm, would march four abreast into the courtroom. It looked as if the defendants were being dragged, though this may have been an illusion produced by their handcuffed state. The sense of brutality would subside only after the officers removed the handcuffs and the defendants took their seats at the defense table. During the unshackling, Borukhova always looked over her right shoulder; Mallayev looked straight ahead. The officers removed prayer books that both defendants held in their handcuffed hands, unlocked and removed the handcuffs, and then returned the books to their owners. In the brief interval between the removal of her handcuffs and the restoration of her prayer book, Borukhova would make the small, economical gesture of kissing her hand to her sisters and mother. During the trial, I often wondered about the conditions in the prisons to which Mallayev and Borukhova returned after the day's proceedings, and one day, after the end of the trial, I went to Rikers Island to see the cells in which they had lived — for thirteen months in Borukhova's case, and eighteen months in Mallayev's. My visit only confirmed the hollowness of the concept of presumption of innocence.

8

O N my way to meet Alla, I would pass Borukhova's mother and sisters, who also ate their lunch in this corridor. I would greet them and they would nod back at me. They had rebuffed my request for an interview, but one day I found the courage to approach them again, to broach a matter I knew must be close to their hearts. This was Borukhova's self-starvation. Since her incarceration, because of her strict religious dietary rules, she had all but stopped eating and had lost an enormous amount of weight. She refused the prison food and had been living on matzos and peanut butter from the commissary. During the pre-trial hearings, Scaring asked Hanophy for an earlier trial date because of Borukhova's continuing weight loss (he was turned down), and now he repeatedly asked that food she could eat be brought to the courtroom; some fruit had been produced, but Borukhova was continuing to starve. The sisters briefly answered my questions, while the mother, who doesn't speak English, looked on. The sisters said that although kosher food was available at Rikers Island, it wasn't on a high enough level of kashruth for their sister to eat. I asked if they could bring her the right kosher food, and they said they wanted to but were not allowed to. They spoke reluctantly and warily. The older sister, Natella Natanova, had reason to watch her words. A year earlier, she had been arrested for threatening Gavriel Malakov, the youngest Malakov son. He accused her of saying, "You know, if you talk, you will be the next to go." She was released on $75,000 bail, tried, and, in the end, acquitted of the charges of tampering with and intimidating a witness. The trial took place in July, 2008, in Queens Supreme Court, and Brad Leventhal was the prosecutor. The sisters were eager to end the talk with me, and I accepted the dismissal. The mother smiled at me once, and I noticed that her front teeth were gold.

9

Borukhova took the stand in midafternoon, and after examining her for two and a half hours, Scaring looked up at Hanophy and said, "Judge, would this be an appropriate time for a recess?"

"Nah," the judge said.

Scaring persisted. "I'm a little tired and I'm afraid the jury might be a little tired too. It's an important witness for me."

"They're doing fine," Hanophy said.

"I'm sorry?"

"They're doing fine. They usually raise their hand if they want something."

"If they raise their hand, then we could quit?"

"No, no. Come on. Let's continue."

I was sitting next to Billy Gorta, and I asked him why the judge would not grant Scaring's request. "The judge is sulking," Gorta said. "He thought summations would be tomorrow. Now this could take days." The pace of the trial had accelerated. Lunch hours and breaks were shorter, the wait at the beginning of the day was less interminable, and, most conspicuously and significantly, the attorneys' requests for sidebar conferences, which had almost invariably been granted in the early days of the trial, were now routinely rebuffed.

"Sidebar" refers to the area beneath and to the side of the judge's bench—the side farthest from the jury box—where the attorneys of both sides gather after one of them receives a yes to the question "May I approach, Your Honor?" The sidebar conference is a form of *pas devant les enfants*. The children (the jurors and spectators) are put out of earshot so that the grown-ups (the attorneys and the judge) can talk about things their charges shouldn't hear. The attorneys' sotto-voce words, however, are not lost to posterity but become a part—often an arrestingly interesting part—of the trial transcript. At sidebar, attorneys step out of the roles they have been playing in open court and become like actors going over the particulars of a night's performance with the director, pointing out each other's lapses, asking for better direction, and sometimes even proposing that the play be closed down — i.e., that a mistrial be called.

On February 17th, for example, during a long sidebar preceding the testimony of the prosecution's fingerprint expert, William Bieniek, Siff complained almost to the point of tears about the judge's treatment of him during his cross-examination of a prosecution witness the previous day. The transcript reads:

> Mr. Siff: . . . There was an unfortunate series of colloquy between yourself and myself in front of the jury which I believe was extremely prejudicial and highly damaging to the defense. The jury, as we have all seen, admires and respects Your Honor. When you talk to them —
> The Court: Rightly so.
> Mr. Siff. Absolutely. They smile, they're forthcoming with you. We have seen their faces and their reactions when you address them and so now there's this danger that has resulted in the fact that you are berating me in front of the jury.
> The Court: I never berated you. I didn't berate you.
> Mr. Siff: Well, that's why —
> The Court: If somebody objects to it and I sustain it that's hardly berating.
> Mr. Siff: I believe it went further than that. It got to the point where Mr. Scaring had to ask for a sidebar.

However, when, a few days later, I talked to Siff — a genial man in his mid-forties, who is married to a retired N.Y.P.D. officer and has two children — he had only praise for Hanophy. "Though I don't agree with all his rulings, I think he's an excellent judge. I've known him for many,

many years. I've known his family for many years. I think he's fair. He's a good man. A gentleman, a kind man, funny. The only thing I see wrong with him he's a Jets fan." Siff told me that Hanophy had handpicked him to defend Mallayev. Normally, Legal Aid lawyers are selected by rotation, but in this case "He actually sought me out, called me in, asked me do I want this case? I said okay."

During Siff's cross-examination of the fingerprint expert, Scaring again asked for a sidebar. The judge was still putting Siff in his place. When the sidebar was granted, Scaring said, "Mr. Siff is asking questions repeatedly that Your Honor is sustaining the objections to. The jury is getting very upset. I'm watching the jury." However, Scaring's concern was not so much for the susceptibilities of his humiliated colleague as for the likelihood that "the jury is going to blend the two of us together." He went on, a bit incoherently, though his meaning was perfectly clear:

> I find it difficult myself to even raise issues with regard to this witness because I don't want to be lumped together with the dissatisfaction that the jury is viewing of the defense lawyer . . . . I don't want to be seen as part of what appears to be obstructionist conduct by Mr. Siff in front of the jury. I would respectfully, Your Honor, ask to have a mistrial so that I can try my own case.

Of course, nothing came of Scaring's request for a mistrial; the judge simply denied it. In his cross-examination of Bieniek, Siff's performance was actually better than it had ever been before in the trial. Much was at stake here. If the expert convinced the jury that the fingerprints on the silencer were indisputably Mallayev's, then there was no hope for Siff's client — or, by extension, for Scaring's. It was Siff's job to try to discredit Bieniek, and he worked manfully to do so — by challenging his credentials, casting doubt on his objectivity, and, most interesting, attacking the whole "science" of fingerprint analysis. He is not the only one to do so; throughout the history of this forensic technique, there have been cases of misidentification and, in the light of them, criticisms of its claim of infallibility. In the past few years, following the outrageous case of an Oregon lawyer named Brandon Mayfield, who was arrested for involvement in the Madrid terrorist bombing of 2004, because his fingerprints appeared to match the latent prints found on a bag of detonators near the attack — and in the end didn't match them at all — these criticisms have increased, and were recently recapitulated in a report by the National Research Council that characterized all forensic techniques (except DNA analysis) as lacking in scientific rigor.

Siff thus had some excellent cards to play in his cross-examination of Bieniek — except that he wasn't able to play them. Whenever he asked Bieniek a question about the Mayfield case or other recorded cases of misidentification, Leventhal would object and Hanophy would sustain the objection. It reached the point where Siff said, "Have you heard about the case — " and Leventhal objected before the name of the case was cited. When Siff protested ("I haven't even mentioned anything about the question, Judge"), Hanophy said, "Is it going to be Curtis Mayfield or whatever the guy's name is?" "Brandon Mayfield," Siff said. "Was that going to be the name?" "No, it wasn't," Siff said with dignity, and cited another case of misidentification, which he wasn't allowed to pursue, either.

When Scaring took over the interrogation of the fingerprint expert, it was like the turn in a master class, when the master shows how it should be done. Bieniek frequently testified at trials, and someone had taught him the technique of looking at the jury when he answered questions. He had conspicuously done so under Leventhal's and Siff's questioning. But when Scaring questioned him, he looked at Scaring like a mouse looking at a cobra. Scaring riveted not only the witnesses' attention but that of the jurors as well, who went from staring dully ahead of them to looking alive and interested. Bieniek (with the help of the judge) had blown Siff off. Now he bowed to Scaring's mastery. His truculence turned to obedience. He made concession after concession. He said what Scaring wanted him to say. "Would you agree that when you do a latent print examination, you should do it without any preconceived notion as to who the person is who allegedly committed the crime?" Scaring asked. "Yes, of course," Bieniek answered. Scaring then confronted him with an earlier admission that he had overheard conversations about the case in his office and knew that cell-phone towers were involved.

Q: There is no report or note that you made that says when you received that information, correct?
A: I never received the information, sir.

Q: Well, you just told us you did. . . .

A: I overheard the information.

Q: Well, if you overheard it you received it, right?

A: No.

Q: Well, if you overheard it you were aware of it, right? Yes?

A: Vaguely.

Q: And if the information would contaminate your identification that would be important to note, correct? Yes? Yes?

A: It wouldn't contaminate my examination.

Q: It won't?

A: No, because I didn't know what it was about.

Q: Well, this case was all over the newspapers wasn't it?

A: It was in the newspapers, yes.

Q: I mean, here you were working on a case that is all over the television, it's over the newspapers — that's true, isn't it? Right?

Mr. Leventhal: Judge, I'm gonna object to this.

Evidently no less mesmerized by Scaring than Bieniek, Hanophy overruled the objection.

The Court: I'll allow it. Go ahead. You may answer.

Q: Yes?

A: I'm sorry, could you —

Q: You're working on a case that's all over the television, it's all over the newspapers, yes?

A: That's true.

When Brandon Mayfield was arrested in Portland, Oregon, on May 6, 2004, it was all over the newspapers that his fingerprints matched the latent prints on the bag of detonators in Madrid and that, moreover, he was a Muslim convert and had defended a terrorist named Jeffrey Leon Battle. Mayfield had defended Battle in a custody case, and not in the criminal trial in 2002, which led to his being sentenced to eighteen years for his participation in terrorist activities — but the distinction didn't seem to matter. In an affidavit supporting the warrant for Mayfield's arrest, a federal agent named Richard K. Werder described in elaborate detail the plots against America that Battle and his fellow conspirators Patrice Lumumba Ford, Ahmed Bilal, Muhammad Bilal, and Maher Hawash confessed to at their trial. He also cited sinister-sounding Muslim organizations in Oregon that Mayfield had associations with. All this on top of the "hundred-percent identification" of his fingerprints made by a senior F.B.I. fingerprint examiner and verified by two other F.B.I. examiners. It didn't look good for Mayfield. It looked like a case of brilliantly realized police work.

When Borukhova was arrested, on February 8, 2008, it looked like a similarly satisfying instance of police know-how. In a story of February 10, 2008, in the Metropolitan section of the *Times,* Al Baker celebrated the triumph of the N.Y.P.D.:

> In a world where no case is a slam-dunk — where investigative gains are measured in the phone calls made, the doors knocked on and the footsteps needed to canvass neighborhoods — and where many leads are dead ends, the answers to Dr. Malakov's death in Queens came in waves of providence for the police. The investigative crumbs seemed to align so well that it would not have even made a good TV show.

Baker cited break after break that had led to the arrest
first of Mallayev and then of Borukhova, and went on to
quote a retired police detective: "It was a house of cards;
that is what it looks like. Everything the detectives did, it
went right. Everything the bad guys did, it went wrong.
And when it started to go, it just fell in the way it was
supposed to."

In the Mayfield case, it did not fall in the way it was
supposed to. The Spanish National Police, who were skep-
tical of the Mayfield identification from the start, presently
produced the fingerprints of an Algerian named Ouhnane
Daoud; these were the right prints. Mayfield was released
from prison (where he had been held in solitary confine-
ment, for two weeks), apologized to, and ultimately paid
$2 million in reparation for his ordeal. The analogy to the
case of Mallayev and Borukhova — for whom no deus ex
machina of exculpatory fingerprints arrived — lies in the issue of contamination. In both cases, were facts known about
the owner of the hundred-percent matching fingerprints
that influenced the judgment of the identifier? Did the F.B.I.
examiners pick Mayfield's prints over the nineteen other
sets of prints spewed out by a computer — which had been
asked to find prints with ridge patterns similar to the latent
prints on the bag of explosives — because they knew he was
a Muslim with connections to terrorists? As Bieniek peered
at Mallayev's prints through his magnifying glass, was he
thinking about the cell-phone calls between Mallayev and
Borukhova that had first put Mallayev under suspicion? Al

Baker's story gives the impression that the police found Mallayev through his fingerprints. But this was not the case. Because of the cell-phone calls, Mallayev was already a suspect when the fingerprints emerged. The police had learned a lot about him — for example, that he was a relative by marriage of Borukhova and that he may have attended the Borukhova-Malakov wedding. The police had not, in fact, escaped the plodding door-to-door work that Baker believed they had been providentially spared. They had (as I later learned from a member of the Malakov family) patiently canvassed the Malakovs to learn the names of all male guests at the wedding, and for any scraps of information about them.

However, even when Scaring cornered Bieniek into admitting that, yes, he knew about the cell towers and, yes, he had read about the case and seen reports of it on television, he must have been aware of the countervailing riptide taking Mallayev out to sea, and Borukhova with him. If an expert says that the prints match, who will dare to say that they don't, even if the chart purporting to show points of matching between a latent and an inked fingerprint — such as the one shown to the jury at the Mallayev and Borukhova trial — shows the untrained eye nothing at all. Bieniek's composure had been ruffled by Scaring, but the authority of his boring and incomprehensible testimony remained intact as he left the stand and, passing the jury box, waved goodbye.

10

THE appearance on the stand of a trim, youngish lawyer named David Schnall marked a turn in the prosecution's narrative; up to this point it had revolved around Mallayev. Leventhal's witnesses had been police officers, eyewitnesses to the shooting, and criminologists whose collective testimony established the Georgia hit man's guilt. Now Leventhal could attend to the evil woman who had hired him. Through Schnall, who identified himself as the court-appointed law guardian of Michelle Malakov, he would return to the navel of the case—the decision by Judge Sidney Strauss that had driven Borukhova to her terrible expedient—and provide an answer to the question of why the judge had taken the child away from the mother and given her to the father. Schnall would introduce and read into the record the remarks that Strauss had made in justification of his ruling.

In a sidebar, Scaring fought hard to prevent this reading from taking place. He said that the prosecutors "want to show that somebody else made a determination that she's a bad person." Hanophy ruled against him. But when Schnall read aloud Strauss's remarks. they did not make Borukhova seem like a bad person at all. They made Strauss seem petulant and irrational. Courts routinely remove children from homes where they are neglected, abused, malnourished, traumatized. I know of no other case where a well-cared-for child is taken from its mother because it sits on her lap during supervised visits with an absent father and refuses to "bond" with him. Yes! The whole of Strauss's reason for his radical ruling was his irritation with Borukhova for "prevent[ing] Michelle from bonding and further strengthening her relationship with her father" during the court-ordered visits at a private agency called Visitation Alternatives, run by social workers. "It was anticipated that through the good offices of Visitation Alternatives perhaps an atmosphere could be created whereby Mr. Malakov could begin to spend some quality time with his four-year-old daughter without any interference or overbearing or for lack of a better word smothering of this child by her mother," Strauss said, and went on to quote from the most recent Visitation Alternatives report on how the visits were going:

> Mr. Malakov constantly greets Michelle with upbeat tone and voice, a smile, and is attempting to hug her. Michelle is not responding to Mr. Malakov's intent to communicate. Michelle does not speak to Mr. Malakov or make eye contact with him. Michelle will cling to her mother who is always carrying Michelle into the visitation. Michelle often buries her head in the mother's shoulder and will turn her body away from Mr. Malakov as he attempts to engage her . . . . She clings to her mother at the onset of the visitation and all attempts to separate her have failed. Michelle will cry hysterically on her mother and becomes incapable of being consoled.

"If there was ever a situation in the mind of this particular Court that cries out for immediate action, it is this, and that which I have just described," Strauss said in conclusion. "Therefore, the Court today without a hearing . . . is directing that the custody of Michelle be immediately turned over to her father, Daniel Malakov, forthwith, if possible." In other words, the solution to the problem of a child who cries hysterically when threatened with separation from her mother while in the presence of her absent father — is to take the child away from the mother and send her to live with the father! Borukhova's shock at the ruling may be imagined. Her matrimonial lawyer, Florence Fass, immediately appealed, but the appeals court upheld Strauss. Borukhova was not the only person shocked by the decision. The social workers had recommended that Borukhova absent herself from the visits so that Malakov could "rebuild his relationship with Michelle." They had not proposed a transfer of custody. Neither had Daniel or his family. But on October 23rd the transfer actually took place, in Khaika Malakov's front yard, where Michelle was pried loose from her mother's arms and carried sobbing into the house.

How had this nightmare — every mother's nightmare — become a reality? What malevolent fairy had written its surreal script? At another court proceeding, Borukhova had identified herself as "a refugee in the United States. I came for freedom of speech and freedom of religion and civil rights as well." What missteps had she made to place herself under state control as powerful and arbitrary as that of the old Soviet regime? What had she misunderstood about her new country that set her on her blundering course toward Strauss and his fateful fit of pique?

At the criminal trial, Borukhova's turbulent marriage to Daniel Malakov was sketched with the lightest of pencils. Neither side ventured into the minefield of accusations Borukhova had made against Malakov of physical violence and child sexual abuse. He was not on trial — she was. He was dead and she was accused of killing him. But from court documents we can follow the itinerary of Borukhova's journey out of the merciful messiness of private life into the pitiless orderliness of the legal system.

Borukhova and Malakov were married in November of 2001, produced Michelle in February, 2003, and separated in November, after he told her — as she reported in several court filings — to get out of the house or "clean the apartment with my tongue." She took the child and went to live with her mother, returning to Malakov a few times, but finally moving out permanently after "I saw the plaintiff kissing Michelle's genitalia in front of me on two separate occasions." On the first occasion, when she confronted him, "he apologized, told me it was his way of showing affection, and promised never to do it again." The second time, Borukhova went on, Malakov "became physically abusive, punching me in and about the head and chest and telling me that, if I called the police, I would be sorry and would never see our daughter again." In her first tentative step into the court system that would swallow her, Borukhova did call the police, but stepped back after Malakov was arrested; like many battered women, she did not press charges. However, on June 24, 2005, citing further abuse, she requested and received a temporary order of protection from the

Queens Family Court, whereby Daniel was ordered to stay away from her and Michelle or be liable to criminal prosecution. Now she had crossed the line between the private and the public. She had asked the state for help and the state had given it, but, in exchange for its protection, had exacted control over a part of her life — her motherhood — that was as firm in its way as the "stay away" directive to Malakov. Henceforth, Michelle would be under the eye of the court; her relations with her father would be monitored by it. Borukhova was ordered to bring Michelle to visits with Malakov, supervised by social workers, who, in turn, were required to send reports to the court on the conduct of the visits.

The court documents do not reveal what was actually going on between Borukhova and Malakov during the disintegration of their marriage. The documents are a crude allegory of ill will peopled by garishly drawn, one-dimensional characters. But some truth leaks out of every court document, as it does out of everything written or said. A document that tells a disconcerting truth about Borukhova is her "counterclaim" to the suit for divorce on the ground of abandonment, filed by Malakov in April of 2005. In the counterclaim, Borukhova demands child support and spousal maintenance, medical insurance, life insurance, occupancy of the "marital apartment," return of wedding gifts and pieces of furniture, and payment of court costs. These demands diminish her; they put her autonomy into question. She was a practicing physician. She could have done what other able-bodied women do who divorce and wish to avoid entanglement with a troublesome mate. They walk away with nothing. But something impelled Borukhova — perhaps her early experience of authoritarianism — to remain in the dangerous game she could have chosen not to play.

She made another unwise move in 2005. She submitted affidavits to the Family Court from two people — a neighbor named Judy Harrypersad and a building porter named Damian Montero — who said that they had seen Malakov sexually molesting Michelle in the basement of her apartment building. In the stately words of the Family Court judge, Charles J. Heffernan, Jr., on whose desk the complaints landed, "Both affidavits state that the affiant saw Daniel Malakov, the Respondent in the above matter, perform or about to perform grave misconduct directed at the vagina of his young daughter." Malakov denied the allegations, and in November, Heffernan held a hearing — called an integrity hearing — on their truth. At the hearing, both witnesses recanted their statements and said the affidavits had been written by Borukhova's sister Natella Natanova, who had bullied them into signing. Under cross-examination, the recanting witnesses acknowledged that they had received threatening phone calls from unidentified males. Heffernan concluded — as he wrote at the end of a letter about the matter he felt constrained to write to the Queens D.A., Richard A. Brown, that "I found, without reservation, that Ms. Harrypersad and Mr. Montero were credible witnesses" and "on the contrary, I found Ms. Natanova's testimony untruthful." Brown did not respond, but Heffernan's finding dealt Borukhova's credibility a severe blow.

Perhaps the most unfortunate consequence for Boru-khova of her application to the Family Court—though it didn't seem ominous at the time—was its appointment of a law guardian for Michelle. In 1962, the New York State Legislature passed a Family Court Act giving children the right to be represented by counsel, and by 2005 it was rou-tine for family courts to assign law guardians to the chil-dren of the warring couples who came before them. The law guardian assigned to look after "the best interests" of Michelle was David Schnall—who almost immediately took against Borukhova and, in effect, acted as a powerful second lawyer for Daniel Malakov in the proceedings now before Sidney Strauss (who took over the case from Heffer-nan in the spring of 2006). Schnall fed and fanned Strauss's fury at Borukhova. After the murder, he vehemently op-posed her attempt to regain custody of Michelle.

I I

W HEN Schnall testified at the criminal trial, I was not yet acquainted with his role as Borukhova's nemesis. Under Leventhal's questioning he emerged as an intelligent and well-spoken representative of a manifestly worthy field of law. During the long sidebar in which Scaring fought to keep Schnall from reading Strauss's "prejudicial" remarks about Borukhova's behavior during the visits, the courtroom was cleared, and as I hovered outside with my fellow evicted spectators, I noticed Schnall sitting on one of the chairs that lined the corridor. I went up to him and asked if Anna Freud's project in the 1960s with Yale law professors and child psychiatrists concerning "the best interests of the child" had been an influence on his work as a law guardian. He said that he didn't know of the project but was interested in hearing about it. I told him that I was writing about the trial and asked if he would be available for an interview.

Journalists request interviews the way beggars ask for alms, reflexively and nervously. Like beggars, journalists must always be prepared for a rebuff, and cannot afford to let pride prevent them from making the pitch. But it isn't pleasant for a grown man or woman to put himself or herself in the way of refusal. In my many years of doing journalism, I have never come to terms with this part of the work. I hate to ask. I hate it when they say no. And I love it when they say yes. Schnall said yes. He said there were things he could tell me about the law-guardian field that would amaze me — dark, bad things — and gave me his phone number. When we were finally readmitted to the courtroom, Leventhal continued his examination of Schnall, who now had permission to read Strauss's remarks, and who continued to appear plausible and neutral.

Scaring's cross-examination followed, and Schnall emerged from it looking less plausible and neutral. Scaring quickly confronted him with a bill he had sent to Borukhova charging her for seven telephone conferences with him that had never taken place — they had been with Malakov. She questioned the bill — but then abjectly paid it, "because you were in a very important position with regard to what occurred to her child; isn't that true?" (The original act of 1962 stipulated that law guardians be paid by the state, but in the early nineties a private-pay category was established whereby law guardians in custody cases would be paid at market rates by parents who could afford their fees. Schnall had been paid the statutory $75 an hour when the case was before Heffernan; when it moved to Strauss, he received permission to charge a private fee of $225 an hour.) Scaring next skewered Schnall on the fact that he had never spoken with the child whose interests he was supposed to be representing. Schnall squirmed and pleaded her youth—he said she was "nonverbal." "Nonverbal when she's four years old? Nonverbal?" Scaring witheringly said. I have since learned that not speaking to their clients is almost a badge of honor among law guardians. In a 1982 study by the New York State Bar Association, this practice was found to be ubiquitous and was deplored; but it remains in place to this day. Recently, in a rare ruling, an appellate judge removed a law guardian from a custody case in Rensselaer County on learning that "he had neither met nor spoken with the child." But judges continue to turn a blind eye to the phenomenon of what the Bar Association study called the "phantom" attorney.

Another revelation came out of Scaring's cross-examination. It seemed that the fatal proceeding of October 3rd took place only because Schnall insisted that it do so. Both Malakov's attorney, Nathan Pinsakov, and Borukhova's attorney, Florence Fass, had wanted an adjournment. But, as

Schnall testified, "I told the judge . . . I would not consent to [the adjournment] because I was very disturbed by the report from Visitation Alternatives describing Miss Borukhova's behavior during the visitation." Scaring bore down:

> Q: And in spite of Daniel Malakov's lawyer saying to you he wanted — didn't want to go to court, wanted to adjourn it, you insisted on going forward, yes?
> A: That's correct.

When I expressed my bafflement about Strauss's ruling to Florence Fass, she nodded and said, "Perhaps we caught the judge on a bad day." I wanted to ask Strauss if he regretted his decision, but he didn't consent to an interview.

12

E ZRA Malakov is two years older than his brother Khaika, and an entirely different physical type: he is short and chunky with an outthrust lower lip that gives his face a pugnacious expression. When he testified for the prosecution, Leventhal asked him what his occupation had been in Uzbekistan and he replied that he had been a dentist for twenty years and then, after winning a singing contest, became a state-employed soloist on radio and television. "And since coming to the United States of America, what do you do?" Leventhal asked in his high voice. "I'm a hazan. I'm a singer in a synagogue. A cantor." Although Ezra had lived in the United States for eighteen years, he had never learned English, so an interpreter relayed Leventhal's questions to him in Russian and then translated his Russian answers into English. When Khaika testified, two weeks earlier, he, too, used an interpreter, though he speaks passable if not fluent English. Under Leventhal's questioning, Khaika reported a threat made by Borukhova's sister Sofya three days before the murder. He said that Sofya said to him and his wife, "Do you know what you've done? You took a child from a mother, and you're going to have a big problem. If you don't give back the child, you are going to lose your child on Sunday."

Ezra was put on the stand to report another threat — this one from Borukhova. Leventhal rubbed his hands as he drew Ezra's account from him: One morning, two or three days before the murder, on the street near his house, Ezra saw a distraught Borukhova, who was talking on a cell phone. He approached her and asked what was troubling her, why she was so anxious and nervous. "What's going on? Maybe I can help you in some way." She put down the phone and said "Daniel took away my child." "If he took away, he will give her back to you," Ezra said soothingly. "No, he will not give the child back to me." "I will help," Ezra said. "I don't need any help," Borukhova said. "His days are numbered. Everything is decided about them."

Scaring had subdued Khaika during cross-examination with his usual practiced badgering. In Ezra he encountered a baffling new creature. There was an amazing moment during Scaring's attempt to corner Ezra over his failure to report Borukhova's threat to the police.

> Q: So we are crystal clear, you never reported this conversation to the police, true?
> A: No, no.
> Q: You did report it to the police?
> A: I did not report to the police. How many times can he say that? I'm a person. I'm a human being, I'm not a child. He asked me this question three times. I'm not a child here. He should ask me in an intelligent, gentle way.

You don't often hear speech like this in a courtroom. Witnesses are willing, sometimes even eager, to play the game of matching wits with an adversary who is sure to defeat them because he is a professional and they are amateurs. Ezra's refusal to play—his continued protests against being questioned in a way people aren't questioned in life outside the courtroom—brought into sharp relief the artificial and, you might even say, inhuman character of courtroom discourse.

13

BORUKHOVA began losing the game very early in her cross-examination by Leventhal. Clearly, nobody had told her not to spar with him. Scaring should have warned her away from exchanges like this one:

Q: Your husband, Mr. Daniel Malakov, he sued you for divorce, didn't he?

A: He applied for divorce.

Q: He sued you for divorce, correct? He filed an action suing you for divorce, correct?

A: He applied for the divorce, yes.

Q: Did you understand my question, ma'am?

A: If you are asking if he applied for divorce, yes, he did.

Q: He brought the action for divorce against you, correct?

A: Correct.

Q: You didn't bring an action for divorce against him, did you?

A: No.

Q: After Daniel sued you for divorce or applied for divorce — to use your term — that was after your daughter had been born, correct?

A: Correct.

Q: And Daniel applied for divorce when your daughter was still an infant, correct?

A: No.

Q: She wasn't an infant?

A: No. It was April '05.

Q: How old was she?

A: She was almost two and a half years old.

Q: That's when he sued for divorce?

A: That's when he applied for divorce, yes.

Leventhal moved on, letting Borukhova have the last word on the "sued" vs. "applied for" debate — and leaving her looking stubborn and evasive. The exchange could be taught in a course on trial technique: it illustrates the way a good cross-examiner, like a good chess player, will inflect long-term strategy with short-term opportunism. Like his quick, darting tread, Leventhal's quick, darting mind instantly grasped the misstep Borukhova had made when she corrected his "sued" with "applied for." He saw the vulnerable pawn that would be his in two or three moves and played them.

Another problem with Borukhova's courtroom performance (during the direct as well as the cross-examination) was her relationship—or nonrelationship—to the jury. Borukhova behaved as if the jury didn't exist—speaking only to her interlocutors—and the jurors, in turn, behaved as if she didn't exist. I watched them not watching her. The whole purpose of putting a defendant on the stand is to influence the jury in his favor. Out in the hallway, during a break in Leventhal's cross-examination, a spectator said to Scaring, "For God's sake, tell her to look at the jury." Scaring replied, "I think that's so phony when they do that." Yes, it looked phony when the fingerprint expert elaborately turned to the jury to answer Leventhal's questions, like an actor addressing the audience over the heads of his fellow actors. The defendant's task is to address the jury over the head of his interrogator without seeming to be doing so. The task is difficult but can be achieved. The defendant can make known his awareness of and regard for the jury in subtle ways. The model might be a person at a party standing in a group and talking to one person, but in such a way as to make the others feel they are part of the conversation. Borukhova acted as if no one were in the room but the person asking her questions.

Leventhal, normally a pleasant person, transformed himself into a deeply unpleasant one for his cross-examination of Borukhova. He was aggressive and accusatory. He could barely conceal his contempt and dislike. He called her Miss Borukhova rather than Dr. Borukhova. Borukhova was sometimes very good at standing up to him. But her intelligence did her no good. As Leventhal relentlessly bore down on her — he interrogated her for two days — she looked increasingly defensive, rigid, stubborn, willful, devious. Leventhal grew harsher and harsher. He was barely civil. "Are you making this stuff up as you go along?" he once permitted himself to say. Scaring objected and the judge murmured a reproof, but it was too late: it had been said. Borukhova wore her white jacket of innocence and kept her head high. She looked regal. She looked like a captive barbarian princess in a Roman triumphal procession. And the jury kept not looking at her.

The most painful part of Leventhal's interrogation had to do with electrocardiograms that had been seized from Borukhova's office after Mallayev's arrest. Mallayev had explained to the police that the ninety-one telephone calls between him and Borukhova between October 3 and October 26, 2007, were doctor-patient calls. He had said that Borukhova was his family doctor and was treating his wife for various ailments — which prompted the Queens District Attorney, Richard A. Brown, to remark, "I don't call my doctor ninety times in the course of two weeks before I see him." (When the police questioned Mallayev about the phone calls, he is reported to have said, "Is there any amount of calls too many to make when it comes to your health?")

In the direct examination, Scaring produced records of Borukhova's treatment of the Mallayevs — in particular that of Mrs. Mallayev, who suffered from a heart condition — to demonstrate that the telephone calls were about medical rather than murderous matters. Leventhal hastened to block this escape route. During Scaring's examination, Borukhova had noted in passing that the dates on the Mallayevs' EKGs were incorrect because the time and date stamp on her electrocardiogram apparatus was not set up. Out of this apparently negligible detail Leventhal fashioned a hideous instrument of torture. One by one he presented Borukhova with thirty-six other of her patients' EKGs, and in each case forced her to concede that the time and date were correct. Only the Mallayevs' EKGs were stamped with the wrong time and date. The torture went on for almost two hours. "I will do this all day," Leventhal said at one point, like a Victorian schoolmaster caning a child until he admits his wrongdoing. "So I will give you the opportunity again, Miss Borukhova, would you like to change your testimony concerning whether or not the date and time stamp on your EKG machine was never set up in your office?" Borukhova stubbornly refused to yield. "Never set up by me," she kept pointlessly equivocating. In the press room, during a break, I overheard Billy Gorta on the phone telling his editor, "The lies are mounting. There was no knockout blow. But she's been cut. She's bleeding."

During his redirect examination, Scaring did what he could to stem the flow. There was an explanation for the Mallayevs' fishy EKGs. The Mallayevs, unlike Borukhova's other patients, were not insured, so Borukhova did their EKGs herself in order to avoid the expense of the technician who did the insured patients' EKGs and who didn't forget to set the time-and-date stamp. All sort of plausible, but too late. She could be making this stuff up, too. And it was not interesting the way Leventhal's torture had been.

In a sidebar during the redirect, Scaring lost another battle with Leventhal. He wanted to question Borukhova about a psychologist named Igor Davidson, who had been treating Michelle during the year before the murder. When Scaring asked Borukhova, "What was Dr. Davidson treating your daughter for?" Leventhal objected, and when Hanophy overruled the objection, he asked for and was granted a sidebar. Davidson had been treating Michelle for symptoms associated with the supervised visits. The child was afraid of the father, and Davidson attributed her fear to the memory of seeing him beat up her mother. Leventhal didn't want the jury to hear this. "Counsel is just merely looking to inflame this jury and to try and prejudice the memory of the victim and to try to paint him into a bad person," Leventhal argued. Scaring retorted, "He painted my client as the villain in this marriage throughout. . . . He painted her as a bad mother. She wouldn't allow any overnight visits. There were reasons why she didn't allow overnight visits." But Hanophy ruled for Leventhal, and the jury never heard Davidson's explanation for why Michelle didn't bond with her nice dad.

Davidson has himself been painted in unfavorable colors — at best as a fool and dupe of Borukhova, at worst as an artful accomplice in her lies. He was not a witness at the criminal trial, but he did testify in the Family Court hearing held after the murder to determine whether the child should go back to Borukhova. His testimony was measured and grave. He spoke of his belief in Borukhova's truthfulness — he did not doubt her accounts of Daniel Malakov's abusiveness — and of the progress he felt he was making with the child in overcoming her fear of her father. He was the one person who actually knew Michelle and could speak from her point of view, but he was disregarded. He is the Kent of this tragedy, in the sense that he may be its most humane spirit — and most helpless bystander.

It has never been clear what, exactly, happened to Michelle after the murder. We know that Borukhova left her with a woman in the playground before going to perform CPR on Malakov, but we hear nothing about her until the evening, when Borukhova's interrogation at the precinct station is over, and she and her sisters are desperately trying to locate the child in the building. The sisters had taken Michelle from the woman in the playground and brought her to the precinct — where she was removed from them by representatives of a city agency called Emergency Children's Services, an arm of the Administration for Children's Services known as A.C.S. Borukhova and her sisters never found the child and left the precinct late at night without being able to obtain information about her whereabouts.

An A.C.S. report, written by two social workers, Martha Martinez and Rashedah L. Goodwine, traces the child's journey into nightmare. Michelle was taken from the precinct and deposited at the house of a paternal relative named Tamara Eliasahuilli. When Martinez made a "home assessment" visit to Eliasahuilli the next day, Eliasahuilli told her that "she did not wish to keep the child" because "her presence in her home posed a potential threat to her own safety, as it remained undetermined who was responsible for the death of Michelle's father." Eliasahuilli proposed that Michelle go to her paternal grandparents, Khaika Malakov and Malka Mushivea, and the proposal was adopted. Michelle was packed off to the paternal grandparents that day. On November 1st, Rashedah Goodwine came out to the Malakov-Mushivea house for another home assessment. When she asked why a police car was parked outside the house, she was told that the family was afraid of "the possibility of retaliation by unknown parties." Another Malakov son, Joseph, who was at the house, "insinuated that child's birth mother Mrs. Borukhova lived less than two blocks away and the proximity was unsettling." The report continues,

Mrs. Mushivea then began to remark on her presumptions regarding how her son was murdered. [Goodwine] cautioned the paternal grandmother from making disparaging remarks with the child Michelle present and suggested that Michelle be taken into another area of the residence. Ms. Mushivea replied that it was "Okay" as Michelle "only spoke Russian." (We know from our interactions with Michelle that she understands a significant amount of English.)

The grandparents proposed that a relative named Ludmila Ford take the child off their hands ("They did not wish to have Michelle reside with them for a long period of time"), and Goodwine left, saying that she would convey the proposal to her supervisors. Martinez was back the next day and reported that "the paternal grandmother wanted to know if the child could be placed with Mrs. Ford 'this evening.'" Meanwhile, something happened that solved the grandmother's problem. Michelle had been taken to an A.C.S. office for a visit with her mother. When Borukhova asked her about a bruise on her cheek, the child replied that "'Dani's mom' hit her." Michelle was then taken to another agency for a "trauma assessment," and, after telling the trauma assessor that she was "not happy where she is staying," she was removed from the grandparents' house and sent into foster care.

While Michelle was undergoing this Dickensian ordeal, the Family Court hearing on which her fate hinged was in session. If Borukhova prevailed—if the judge found there was no "imminent risk" in her being returned to Borukhova's care—the ordeal would be over, and Michelle would be sleeping in her own bed again. But, after six days of testimony, the judge, Linda Tally, ruled that there was imminent risk — that the charge of "emotional neglect" leveled by A.C.S. was substantiated — and that the child should remain in foster care. Borukhova, who had cried throughout the hearing, left the courthouse empty-handed. If she had ordered her husband's execution to get her daughter back, she had done so in vain.

14

FLORENCE Fass, an attractive, spirited, and talkative woman in her early sixties, represented Borukhova at the Tally hearing. "Here's what I think was really going on," she told me in her law office in Garden City, a few days after the end of the criminal trial. "I think that the police suspected Mazoltuv. They assumed she would disappear if she was the murderess. 'So how are we going to keep her here? We'll just take the child. The mother's not going anywhere. The mother won't leave her child.' And she didn't. That's what I think was going on. No one will ever be able to prove it. But that's exactly what happened. So between October and February, when the police are putting the case together, the kid is spending her time in foster care." She went on, "I think it was such a travesty of justice. It almost makes you look at the profession in a different way. The way a litigant might. This case was so screwed up. Everything you did was twisted. The law didn't apply to you, somehow. And even today, with this latest motion on Schnall. This motion in any other context would have been a home run. It would have been the judge calling us into chambers and going, 'Look, David, you know I think you ought to step down.' It's not going to happen and I'm probably going to lose the motion."

What motion? I have let Fass run on too long, and have got ahead of my story. Let me go back to my talk in the hallway with the law guardian, who had said yes to an interview. I called him a few days later and he agreed to meet with me on Sunday, March 1st, at three in the afternoon. But on Friday, February 27th, I found a message from him on my answering machine saying that he was canceling the interview "for the time being," because he was "not comfortable talking about the case while it's still in court." He added that he might be willing to talk after the trial was over, and left two telephone numbers. Taking the proviso and the phone numbers as a door left ajar, I called one of the numbers and left a message asking him to call me. At eleven o'clock the next morning, Schnall returned my call. I said I understood his reluctance to talk with me while the trial was going on and looked forward to speaking with him when it was over. Schnall said that talking later would depend on the verdict. If Borukhova wasn't convicted, he wasn't sure about an interview.

I expected the conversation to end there, but instead Schnall began to talk about the case that he said he wouldn't talk about, and I began to take notes. He said, "I'm hoping for a guilty verdict," and added that Leventhal "had mentioned that their case is tough." He spoke of other court hearings at which he had seen "what this woman would do." He talked about his work as a law guardian — "I take the job relatively seriously" — and about the problem of payments. He explained that both parents in custody battles are required to pay the law guardian, but that only one side actually does. "The side I'm disparaging doesn't pay." He added that in the Borukhova case "they tried to get me removed" and made "personal attacks on me." But, he went on, in a new tone of voice, "my real passion isn't family law."

Then he spoke for almost an hour, almost without pause, about the world as a place of hidden evil under the control of "a Communist-like system." "Everything we know to be true isn't true," he said. In a torrent of words, he revealed the truths he had become privy to since "I started this alternate path seven years ago." I reproduce below some of what I scribbled in my notebook from his monologue.

Banks do not lend money. They have no money.
All of the banks are zombie banks.
This is all one shell game.
The system is run by useful idiots.
We need enemies.
There will be genocidal austerity.
There is no energy crisis. There is plenty of oil.
Joseph McCarthy was right.
We've been living under the ten planks of the Communist Manifesto. We're a Communist country.
Orwell's father was a big technocrat.
The powers that be are on a roll.
The phony global-warming agenda.
The nature of the medical profession. All the therapies are not meant to help you, they're meant to harm you.
Polio vaccine doesn't cure polio.
The male sperm gene is down seventy-five percent. We're almost completely sterile.

Everything I've said is not opinion, it's fact. THEY control the world.

If I went public they'd come after me. I already feel my days are numbered. The I.R.S. came to my apartment with summonses three times. The problem is they have guns.

Same thing with 9/11, same thing with Katrina.

"It was known ahead of time?" I interrupted. "Of course," he replied. "I could talk about this for twenty minutes. I could give you so much more on it. Supposedly FEMA was incompetent. They did what they had planned to do."

What was the 1812 war about? Do they teach us that we lost the revolutionary war?

We funded the Soviets.

It's laughable. Once you see it, it's so predictable.

I'm fascinated by how stupid people are. We could talk about Freud, Einstein. There's always a story behind a story. Nobody wants to talk about it. It's time now.

Sacred mysteries of Egypt.

Earth worship. Al Gore quackery.

There's a control grid in place. We're completely monitored. We're contributing to our own demise. Because we're so stupid.

The police — a private army for a private company called the City of New York. That's not hyperbole. That's fact. It's amazing and brilliantly done.

I brought the call to an end after fifty minutes — Schnall had by no means exhausted his esoteric knowledge, but I had heard enough — and sat and thought. Then I did something

I have never done before as a journalist. I meddled with the story I was reporting. I entered it as a character who could affect its plot. I picked up the phone and called Stephen Scaring's office.

Scaring called back an hour later (I had left a message with his secretary saying I had information about a witness). I told him about Schnall's call, and he asked me to fax him my notes. The following Monday, when the judge entered the courtroom, the attorneys clustered around him, each holding a copy of a document. The document was a motion that Scaring had drafted after receiving my fax. It asked "for leave to recall the prosecution witness David Schnall for further cross-examination, and to question Mr. Schnall concerning his mental health, and in particular whether he suffers from paranoid and/or delusional beliefs or perceptions which may affect his reliability and credibility as a witness." The motion quoted from my notes recording Schnall's "beliefs in various strange and ominous conspiracy theories," and cited legal precedents for impeaching the testimony of witnesses who are nuts. "Keep it low," the spectators heard the judge say to Leventhal, who was speaking excitedly in his high voice and making his characteristic agitated gestures. Leventhal, we learn from the transcript, was beside himself over the motion. "Mr. Scaring's motion is absurd," he said to Hanophy. "To suggest that Mr. Schnall because he has certain opinions or possesses certain opinions or beliefs regarding history or regarding the world and its current affairs or any of the beliefs that are illustrated or set forth in Mr. Scaring's motion that he should then be permitted to recall him for purposes of cross-examining him about possible psychiatric issues is — it's just — it's absurd. It's absurd."

Scaring said, "I'm surprised that the prosecution dismisses this so quickly. There is no question when you read that that you realize Mr. Schnall is delusional. Now, nobody holds the beliefs that — " Hanophy cut in, "What, that there really is no energy shortage, there's millions of gallons — " The colloquy continues:

Mr. Scaring: That the government planned or was aware of 9/11.

The Court: How about the one about there's no energy shortage, there's gas and there's oil?

Mr. Scaring: Do you believe, Your Honor, that there's any evidence to suggest that the government was aware of 9/11?

The Court: Do you think that there is a shortage of oil in this world?

Mr. Scaring: Judge, that is one of his statements. There are numerous statements that are clearly delusional. . . . The things that he says make no sense. They're bizarre, they're absurd. And so for the prosecution to quickly assign an absurd word for my motion — the term absurd —

The Court: Right. Your motion is denied.

The jury was brought in and Leventhal produced a few more witnesses, among them the F.B.I. language specialist who translated the *padayesh* phrase as "Are you going to make me happy?" At the end of the afternoon, after a foren-

sic pathologist had testified about his postmortem examination of Daniel Malakov, while Leventhal showed the
jury gruesome pictures of the corpse, the judge turned ex-
pectantly to him and Leventhal said, "People rest." The
next day, Scaring put on four defense witnesses, and made
his shocking midafternoon announcement that Borukhova
would testify. He examined her for the rest of the day. The
next two days, Wednesday and Thursday, were occupied by
Leventhal's brutal cross-examination, and when it was
over, the jury was dismissed, and the judge made an announcement as shocking as Scaring's. He said, "We should
be able to get two summations in tomorrow."

15

IT is time to introduce a subject known as The Judge's
Vacation. Billy Gorta's comment that the judge was
sulking because Scaring put Borukhova on the stand was
part of a discourse with which our journalists' cohort had
entertained itself for several weeks. We talked a lot about a
comment the judge had made during the voir dire to the
effect that the trial would have to end by St. Patrick's Day
(March 17th) — because that was the day he was going on
vacation. As February turned into March, the vacation began to hover over the proceedings. The rumor that the vacation would be in the Caribbean was ascertained to be hard

fact. Scaring recalled the judge saying, "This trial is going to be over on March 17th because I'm going to be sipping piña coladas on the beach in St. Martin." This agreeable prospect was evidently on Hanophy's mind when he curtly denied sidebars, chastised attorneys for latenesses that had previously gone unremarked, and kept the court in session long past the usual 5 P.M. ending hour.

Summations had been expected to begin Monday, March 9th, which left eight days until the vacation. But on March 5th the judge ordered Scaring and Siff to deliver their summations the next day, a Friday. (The order of the opening statements had been Leventhal, Siff, and Scaring; the order of the summations was Scaring, Siff, and Leventhal.) "We are on a very tight schedule," Hanophy said twice. Because both Borukhova and Mallayev were Orthodox Jews, who could not travel after sundown on Friday, Fridays had never before been trial days. It was winter, and the sun went down early. However, now that time was of the essence, Friday, March 6th, became a trial day; the defense summations would start at nine in the morning and end well in time for the defendants' return by daylight to Rikers Island. The prosecution would sum up on Monday. Scaring expressed his outrage. He said he could not possibly prepare his summation in the few evening hours that remained after a long drive to his home, in Huntington, Long Island. "Very nice homes out there," the judge said. "I can't do it," Scaring said. "I am not physically able to put this summation together in this long case now. It's going to be five before we get out of here. It's not fair to my client. I can't do a proper job by tomorrow morning." "Sure you can," the judge said. "I cannot." "Come on, you've been in this business thirty years, you can do it."

Scaring pleaded with Hanophy. He asked for Sunday as a trial day. The judge said no. He proposed that "if the jury deliberation goes beyond the time that Your Honor is here, I believe we consent to having another judge sit in on it." But Hanophy did not want to be sipping piña coladas while another judge sat in his chair and held out his hand for the jury's verdict. He was determined that summations begin the next day. Scaring then argued that if he and Siff had to sum up on Friday, so should Leventhal: it would be the height of unfairness to give Leventhal the whole weekend to prepare while he and Siff had only a few hours. Whether Leventhal summed up on Friday hinged on whether Mallayev and Borukhova could be persuaded to violate their religious laws and stay past sundown. At first, Borukhova demurred, saying she would stay only if she could spend Friday night in the courthouse. When the judge said that was impossible, she agreed to stay if she could be back at Rikers Island by midnight. Mallayev agreed to the same arrangement. The judge asked both of them to say aloud what their attorneys had said for them, and they did. "All right, then," he said, "everybody can sum up tomorrow." However, everybody did not sum up on Friday. On Friday morning, Hanophy murmured something about being "overly cautious" because "appellate issues" could arise if the defendants were allowed to break the Sabbath — and only Scaring and Siff summed up that day. Leventhal got the weekend to prepare.

During Thursday's tense colloquy, the spectators who had lingered in the courtroom saw a sight at the defense table they had never seen before. For the first time in the entire course of the trial, Borukhova and Mallayev were speaking to each other. Neither had ever before made the slightest acknowledgment of the other's presence. Now they were heatedly (though inaudibly) arguing. Alla Lupyan-Grafman later told me that Borukhova had "cut her own throat and her attorney's" in the backstage drama that developed during the onstage agon between Scaring and Hanophy. The judge had offered Scaring and Siff a way out. If Borukhova and Mallayev would agree to break the Sabbath the following Friday and Saturday — in the event that the jury had not yet reached a verdict — he would defer defense summations until Monday the ninth. "Mallayev said yes, right away," Alla said. "But Borukhova said no. She said, 'I'd rather die.' She said to Mallayev, 'Misha, don't you understand that it's a test?' Meaning that God is testing them. And then I said — I know it was not my place to get involved — but I said, 'Marina, if this is not a life-and-death situation, then what is?' And Steve told her, 'I need the time, I can't close tomorrow, it won't be the quality that I need to deliver, not the quality you expect from me. We're finishing late today. I have just one night, there's no way. And the prosecution will close on Monday. They get that advantage.' So he put all the cards in front of her. And she said 'No, I'd rather die.' Then all of a sudden she agrees to stay late the next day. It was so illogical. She was so irrational. Why would you agree to break the Shabbat for sure when the following weekend is hypothetical — ninety-nine percent it won't happen? And to put your attorney in such a terrible position, basically signing your death warrant?"

16

WHEN Alla said this, I had a feeling of déjà vu. I recognized a tone I had heard in the voices of the therapists, police officers, social workers, lawyers, and relatives who testified against Borukhova. The tone was a mixture of disbelief and disapproval. How can she be this way? She shouldn't be this way. Borukhova's otherness was her defining characteristic. With the exception of Igor David-son, at the Family Court hearing, and two hospital colleagues, at the criminal trial, everyone questioned about Borukhova expressed a primal unease that often had nowhere to go except into hostility. Sidney Strauss was not alone in his preternatural anger and impatience. David Schnall seemed to fear and hate her from the start of his guardianship. When Jolie Rothschild, a social worker who became the proprietor of Visitation Alternatives in May of 2007, testified at the Family Court hearing, she couldn't disguise her antipathy. Borukhova's way of getting under people's skin and setting off serious allergic reactions was illustrated with special vividness by the testimony, also at the Family Court hearing, of a court-appointed clinical psychologist named Paul Hymowitz. The perverse imp ordering Borukhova's affairs brought this powerful antagonist into her life not through the intervention of the state but via the well-meaning interference of her own lawyer, Florence Fass. "When Mazoltuv came to me, in July, 2007," Fass told me, "I knew this was a case totally out of control. We do things differently here in Nassau County. We take situations like this and throw in mental-health professionals — it's like triage. We immediately get social workers involved, as well as law guardians, as well as parent coordinators. So when I came into the case, I could not understand for the life of me why forensics had not been ordered — that is, the psychological evaluation of the parties and the child. On the first day I appeared before Judge Strauss, I made the request. Why hadn't anybody — the law guardian, anybody — asked for forensics? Strauss ordered them right there and then with a Dr. Hymowitz, who is used extensively in Queens."

Hymowitz's testimony, perhaps more than any other witness's, buttressed the A.C.S.'s charge of "emotional neglect," whereby a child may be removed from its mother by the state. He began his psychological evaluations of the mother, father, and child in August, 2007, seeing Borukhova and Malakov separately in alternating sessions, and then seeing Michelle and Borukhova together. His first interview with Borukhova made him immediately suspicious of her. The things she told him "were kind of hard to believe," he testified under questioning by the A.C.S. lawyer Eric Perlmutter. Borukhova told Hymowitz that Daniel beat her and sexually molested Michelle, and, hardest of all for him to credit, "she recalled strange ideas [Malakov] had, such as when she was attempting to breast-feed and then bottle-feed the child in the first year when they were living together, he would insist on withholding nurturance, nourishment for eight to ten hours at a time to train the child." Borukhova's account of "the amount of hours that he would go without wanting to feed the child seemed to strain logic," Hymowitz said, and added, "The description of the molestation of the child, again, seemed kind of gruesome and outlandish."

Malakov's interview went better. Hymowitz characterized him as "a gentle, sensitive father who seemed to be very distressed and genuinely emotionally pained about the loss of unencumbered contact with the child." Malakov described Borukhova, Hymowitz said, as "a very irrational, unstable, violently inclined woman." When Perlmutter asked Hymowitz if he had spoken to Malakov about "the concerns raised by the respondent mother," Hymowitz replied that "he was very dismissive of the concerns," and told him that after an investigation by a state agency "the results had come back unfounded."

When Borukhova brought Michelle to Hymowitz's office in mid-October, the encounter further hardened Hymowitz against Borukhova. The four-and-a-half-year-old child wanted nothing to do with the good doctor:

The child was barely looking at me, nonresponsive verbally to anything I said. She was whispering to the mother, most of that communication in Russian, and sitting rather rigidly in the room without approaching the toys or the activities. . . . Once we suggested that mom would leave the room, the child was whining, grabbing the mother, and it just didn't sound like it was going to fly. . . . I can't think of any other case where I could not get the child to stay with me in the office alone.

Hymowitz concluded from Michelle's behavior that she was "rather immature and somewhat regressed." In answer to Perlmutter's question "What did you attribute the child's behavior to?" Hymowitz didn't immediately blame Borukhova. He conceded that she had tried to encourage the child to interact with him. "She was saying and doing the right things." However, "she didn't firmly insist that the child allow her to leave. She did not set certain other limits with the child, now that I'm remembering. For example, the child stood on my couch with her shoes on. I had to ask the mother to have her stop doing that."

Schnall, who appeared at the hearing as law guardian, evidently didn't think that Perlmutter had pushed Hymowitz hard enough on Borukhova's unfitness as a mother. When his turn came to question the psychologist, he was almost gleeful in his acrimony. "Would it be fair to say," he asked Hymowitz, "that she exhibited sociopathic qualities and traits?" Hymowitz replied that at first he wasn't sure "whether we're talking about someone who was delusional, namely out of touch with reality at least in selected areas concerning the child and the father, or whether it was sociopathic and therefore more premeditated and manipulative." After further sharp prodding by Schnall, Hymowitz said, "Having met with her by now well into late October, I began to feel that it was more likely that the behavior was premeditated, manipulative, and with callous disregard not only for the rights of the co-parent but the well-being of the child . . . . It began to seem more premeditated, more coherent in its fabric and less delusional." Schnall wanted still more. "So essentially the mother was lying without conscience?" he said. After a volley of objections by Fass and reformulations by Schnall, the judge allowed this exchange:

> Schnall: So it would be fair to say the mother has been lying without conscience with respect to the ramifications to the father and his relationship with the child?
> Dr. Hymowitz: Yes.

Fass did what she could to contain the fire she had innocently set when she threw in this flammable mental-health professional. "Now, you stated that the father appeared to be a gentle person?" she asked him.

> Dr. Hymowitz: Yes.
> Mrs. Fass: Okay. Did that influence your opinion that the mother's allegations of physical abuse were hard to believe?
> Dr. Hymowitz: Yes.
> Mrs. Fass: Did you ever evaluate someone in a domestic violence case?
> Dr. Hymowitz: Well, yes. Domestic violence is often raised in custody evaluations so I have made those determinations.
> Mrs. Fass: And in any of those evaluations, has the alleged abuser appeared to be a gentle person?
> Dr. Hymowitz: I suppose so.

When examining Borukhova later that day, Fass returned to the point. "Now, Dr. Borukhova, you've heard Dr. Hymowitz describe Daniel as a gentle man. Do you recall that testimony?"

> Dr. Borukhova: This is what everybody said. That he was gentle and, you know, I mean, he was charming and he helped patients. He didn't get money from patients . . .
>
> But, when he used to come home, I mean, he was a totally different person and nobody would believe that somebody could be so different.

"Daniel appeared to be this wonderful person in the community — and apparently he was," Fass told me in her office. "And when he came home he was not. It was like Dr. Jekyll and Mr. Hyde."

Fass's only other witness at the Family Court hearing was Igor Davidson, whose testimony Schnall fought fiercely to discredit. Davidson introduced an element into the hearing that had been entirely absent from it: ambiguity. Alone among the participants, Davidson spoke as if he were in touch with life as it exists outside the courtroom, where everything isn't always this or that, but can be both. When Fass asked him whether he approved of Michelle's placement with the elder Malakovs after the murder, he said, "I didn't believe it was the optimal placement for the child. No." And went on:

> This was really a time where she needed those people and places that were familiar to her and that she could rely on,

that she has sought out in the past for comfort and reassurance. And I was concerned that those were not available to her.

My heart broke for the Malakov family when I heard that this happened. However, I understood that they were grieving, that they were mourning, and in terms of Michelle, I didn't know how many resources they would have available to nurture her or to coddle her, to provide all that attention and all that nurturing that she needed at a time like this.

Davidson's expression of compassion for the elder Malakovs coupled with his imaginative grasp of their conflicted feelings toward Michelle was a remarkable moment in a proceeding dominated by finger-pointing and blaming and punctuated by irritable sparring over evidentiary issues. Another display of Davidson's fine-mindedness came when Schnall confronted him with his affidavit of April, 2007, recommending the temporary cessation of Michelle's visits with the father, after an incident in which Michelle was forcibly removed from the arms of her mother by Malakov and a Visitation Alternatives caseworker and taken into Malakov's house for a supervised visit. She cried hysterically for twenty minutes but eventually subsided and played with her father and seemed happy to be with him. Schnall triumphantly cited the Visitation Alternatives report: "Michelle and the father were smiling and laughing. Michelle engaged verbally with her father. They played with various toys. When Mr. Malakov went into the kitchen, Michelle followed him. She held his hand. Gave him a hug." (Schnall invented the hug, but gave an otherwise accurate account of the Visitation Alternatives report.) Davidson commented, "Twenty minutes of tantrumming seemed excessive to me." Schnall said, "Doesn't it seem odd that she would have such a tantrum and then engage with the father like they never lost any time?" Davidson replied, "It doesn't seem odd. No. No." How then, Schnall sneered, would Davidson account for the disparity between "her initial discomfort" and the laughter and smiles. Davidson replied:

> It's not a disparity at all. I think that you can get used to any situation. It doesn't necessarily mean that it's a healthy and good situation for you to be in.

Schnall dropped the subject. In his testimony Davidson said that when Borukhova told him that Daniel had physically abused her and sexually abused Michelle, he believed her, but he made an important distinction: he was treating the child not for sexual abuse but for the trauma of witnessing domestic violence. He acted on the assumption that the child feared her father because she had seen him hit her mother. This is why she shrank from him during the visits and was producing symptoms (such as bed-wetting and fear of leaving the house) connected with the visits. Davidson said he was working with the child, using behavioral techniques, to dispel her fear and make a relationship with her father possible.

Here we come to another of the questions about Borukhova that blur her portrait and give it its strange tinge.

Why did she keep harping on the sexual abuse? If Daniel's "grave misconduct directed toward his young daughter's vagina" (or what Fass called "inappropriate touching") actually occurred, it surely wasn't the cause of the child's fear of him. Once Heffernan dismissed the affidavits of Judy Harrypersad and Damian Montero as false, and wrote his letter to the D.A., Borukhova would have done well to move away from this disquieting subject. Even if the "esteemed orthodontist" (as Daniel was called in the press) was in fact a closet pervert, it was impolitic of her to continue to go on about it. Her attempt to prove it through witnesses had not only failed but tainted the allegation itself. It would have served her better — it would have been rational and logical — to connect Michelle's fearful, clinging behavior during the visits to scary scenes of domestic violence. If Borukhova had made these scenes vivid for the social workers and the judge, they might not have been so quick to blame her for the failure of the visits. If Strauss's imagination had been stirred by the image of a woman being beaten as a frightened child watches, he might have found another explanation than maternal "smothering" for Michelle's behavior during the visits.

This is only one of many "what if"s by which this tragedy is marked. Another has to do with the arrival of Jolie Rothschild at Visitation Alternatives. What if this imperious, tough social worker had never entered the story? The report from Visitation Alternatives that so inflamed Sidney Strauss was written in the wake of a quarrel between Borukhova and Rothschild, in which Borukhova threatened to sue Rothschild, and was itself full of fury and dislike. What if a conciliatory letter to Rothschild that Borukhova wrote after the quarrel and faxed to Visitation Alternatives hadn't gone astray, like the letter that goes fatally astray in *Tess of the D'Urbervilles*? No one reading the letter—Fass showed me a copy of it—could feel that Borukhova was sabotaging the efforts of the social workers. Indeed, she sounds rather like a social worker herself as she proposes a meeting to "discuss a plan to make Michelle's separation from me during visitations less stressful" and "to recreate the positive atmosphere which we had developed only a few weeks ago." She points out, "I was also the one who suggested that we all sit on the floor and play together," and "This seemed to be working, and I was very optimistic that Michelle was becoming more comfortable with the visits." The letter ends, "Thank you and I hope we can continue to move forward." Rothschild said she never received the letter, and it was never admitted into evidence.

17

O N Friday morning, after a night of almost no sleep, Scaring started his summation bravely, but his tiredness soon showed. He fumbled and couldn't find documents. He lost the thread of his argument. The transcript records the cruel effects of his sleep deprivation.

She says that — one point — excuse me. Now, moving to the CPR. She says that she sees Dr. Borukhova — I know it's long but I'm going to be a little while so bear with me. You know, I don't mind if you nod off but not for the whole thing, okay? Lost my train — forgot what I was talking about. I think I was talking about Ortiz. In any event — oh, the CPR. Thank you very much. Didn't get a lot of sleep last.

Scaring roused himself and the courtroom when he banged loudly on a table and said, "Can you hear that?" and banged again and again said, "Can you hear that?" He was mimicking a piece of theater that Leventhal had performed during his cross-examination of Borukhova to emphasize the suspiciousness of her statement to the police that she had not heard the shots that killed Daniel. Scaring went on to argue that this statement (comparable in its strangeness to Borukhova's accusation against Malakov of withholding milk from the infant) was true precisely because it was so incredible. "If she was guilty, why would she say that?" Scaring said. "She's got to be stupid and she isn't stupid. Why do I want to make myself look suspicious if I'm guilty of this conspiracy? I know he's gonna be shot. . . . It's actually the strongest evidence of her truthfulness, because if she was a liar she would say something that made more sense. I mean, it makes no sense."

But Scaring's exhaustion kept interfering with his attempt to persuade the jury to acquit Borukhova. "I lost my train on that." "I'm sorry. Organization is not my strongest suit." "Excuse me, I'm going to suck on one of these for a minute." "I'm losing my voice so soon I'm going to sit down." His summation was a short, tattered, sad affair. Siff followed with a very long speech. He did not seem the worse for his sleepless night — he is twenty years younger than Scaring — but his summation was as ineffectual as his opening statement had been. Some compelling points he made — that the case against Mallayev started with the cell-phone records and not with the fingerprints, for example — sank into the morass of his long-windedness.

On Monday morning, the benches on the Malakov side of the aisle were overflowing with members of the clan, who had come to hear their well-rested white knight's summation. Leventhal and Aldea, both dressed in dark suits, sat side by side at their table, like a pair of crows imperturbably looking down on carrion. Orderly piles of transcripts and four bottles of water were precisely lined up in front of them. Leventhal's summation was two hours long and even more artful than his opening statement. He began with the words "He took my child. It's already been decided. His days are numbered." After a pause for effect, he repeated Ezra Malakov's words. The summation was a rousing reprise of the prosecution's case, like the parade of the animals and performers at the end of the circus. Leventhal displayed his witnesses against Mallayev, among them "brave, alert, conscientious, and focused" Cheryl Springstein, who had seen the shooting and identified Mallayev in a police lineup; Marisol Ortiz, who had been in Malakov's dental office with her daughter, and had seen him walk toward the playground with Michelle; Rafael Musheyev, a butcher from Samarkand, at whose Flushing apartment Mallayev unexpectedly appeared with his son Boris three days before the murder (Leventhal enacted the scene: "Hey, you mind if me and Boris crash here?") and from which the two disappeared on the day of the murder; Bieniek, the fingerprint expert; Detective Edward Wilkowski of the Queens homicide squad, who arrested Mallayev in Georgia, and to whom he lied about where he was on October 28th until confronted with cell-tower records showing that he was in Queens. "The evidence against Mikhail Mallayev," Leventhal said, "is overwhelming."

But Mallayev wasn't interesting to Leventhal. He dropped the unappetizing hit man from his maw and loped toward his more delectable prey:

> Standing alone he has no motive to murder Daniel Malakov. But, ladies and gentlemen, he doesn't stand alone, he stands with her, the woman who mysteriously tapes their meeting in May of 2007, the woman whom each time, ladies and gentlemen, I submit to you we prove that they are together both in May and again in November, right after they meet this defendant Mikhail Mallayev deposits almost $20,000 in cash into multiple bank accounts.

Leventhal's wobbly syntax reflects the instability of the pillar on which this element of his case against Borukhova rested. He had no proof that the deposits of $20,000 came from her; evidence of money passing between Borukhova and Mallayev did not exist. All there was to suggest that the "paid assassin" had been paid by her was, in the case of the deposit in May, the mysterious tape, and, in the case of the November deposit, Mallayev's name on a calendar that the police had seized from Borukhova's medical office. Of course, the ninety-one cell-phone calls, coupled with motive, were enough to convict Borukhova. But Leventhal was letting no opportunity to buttress his case go by. He knew that juries want more than evidence to convict; they want to be certain that the person they are sending to prison or to another world is an evil creature as well as an evil-doer. So Leventhal worked to blacken the image of Borukhova to the point where the jury could feel good about a conviction. He repeated Judge Strauss's angry words — "If there was ever a situation in the mind of this particular Court that cries out for immediate action it is this and that which I have just described" — and went on to draw this portrait of her:

> A woman who threatened to sue the social workers at Visitation Alternatives. A woman who had problems with David Schnall. A woman, I submit to you, who had problems with anybody that didn't see it her way. A woman who had problems with anybody who didn't agree with her. But I submit to you, ladies and gentlemen, that David Schnall saw her for who she was, the same person —

Scaring objected here and was sustained. But there was plenty of blacking paste left. Leventhal went on to mock the fishy EKGs. He did not scruple to quote (several times) the "Are you going to make me happy?" version of the *padayesh* quotation. He scored a delicious triumph when he showed (with records from Delta Airlines) that Mallayev was in Israel when Borukhova said he and his wife came to her office in the summer of 2007. "If she's lying about that, what else is she lying about?" Leventhal said. He returned to the afternoon, nineteen days earlier, when a stunned courtroom had watched a videotape documenting the transfer of Michelle from her mother's custody to her father's.

The film began in Borukhova's apartment and showed Borukhova with Michelle, tossing a ball in the air and reading to her. Then Borukhova said, "Now we're going to see Daniel," and the child began to cry. Borukhova went on, "Nobody will hurt you. Nobody will do anything to you. Let's go. Let's go outside." The child's crying increased. "You will stay there a few days and then you'll come back, Michelle." The child began to scream. For almost an hour, we heard the child scream until she was hoarse, as she was carried for several blocks down a street and, finally, pulled out of her mother's arms by Daniel and taken into Khaika Malakov's house.

The film was horrifying. Tears came to many eyes. Some of the jurors cringed. Borukhova had commissioned it after seeing a public relations consultant and presenting to him her ideas for protesting the Strauss decision — she would write to Hillary Clinton, for example, or go to Washington with Michelle and sit on the White House lawn. The consultant didn't think much of these frail schemes, but he approved the idea of documenting the transfer and gave her the name of a filmmaker. Borukhova said she wanted to show that "there was a lot of discrepancy between what Visitation Alternatives is writing and the actual things which is going on." The film showed, with unsparing force, the misery of a child being taken away from her mother against her will. It should have been Borukhova's ace in the hole for gaining sympathy from the jury. But, incredibly, Leventhal was able to turn the film against her. He made it seem as if the child had been traumatized not by the transfer itself but by the mother's callous filming of it. The pain that the jurors had felt while watching the film — and I watched them looking afflicted; they weren't playing with their hair or staring into the middle distance — was turned against Borukhova rather than against the judge who had caused it. She would have done better to write to Hillary and sit on the White House lawn.

Leventhal saved for last an ingenious plot twist. He came back to Borukhova's insistence that she didn't hear the shots.

> Mr. Scaring asked you about why would she lie about not hearing those shots. Why would she lie about that? . . . Ladies and gentlemen, she didn't hear the shots because she wasn't there.

According to Leventhal's theory, Borukhova was late for the meeting in the playground because she was fussing with a button spy camera she had bought the day before (to document the killing and use the film against Mallayev "in case he double-crossed her"), trying to follow the instructions to make it work but unable to do so, and finally abandoning the camera and rushing to the playground — only to find that Malakov had already been shot. And here is Leventhal's cleverest stroke: "She said that she didn't hear the shots because she didn't expect to hear any shots. I'll say that again. She said that she didn't hear any shots because she never expected to hear any shots because she knew he was going to use a silencer."

18

THE jury began its deliberations on the afternoon of Leventhal's summation, was sequestered overnight, and came back with a verdict the next day, after lunch. During the six hours of deliberating the jurors sent six or seven notes asking for documents (and coffee in one case). The courtroom was packed. Our little press contingent had been booted out of the front-row seats to make way for police detectives and functionaries from the D.A.'s office. The Malakov side of the aisle was filled with a crush of relatives and friends. On the Borukhova side, to which some of the Malakovs had been obliged to overflow, the mother and sisters were reading aloud from their prayer books in fervent whispers; Mallayev's daughter was davening. The news that the jury had a verdict had come, but the judge did not send for the jurors. He sat serenely surveying the scene. He was waiting for the father. "Tell him I want him in here now," Hanophy finally said. Khaika Malakov entered, and the jury was summoned.

The foreman announced a verdict of guilty for both defendants on all counts of murder in the first and second degrees. The defendants listened expressionlessly. Borukhova said something to Scaring. The jubilant Malakovs filed out of the courtroom. In the hall they hugged Leventhal and the police officers. "God bless America," and "Thank you, America," they said, on the courthouse steps. Khaika told newspaper and television reporters, "Before, I thought the system of justice was not so good. Now I understand the system is high class." The jury had been spirited out of the courthouse — but reporters were able to stake out a few jurors at their homes, and quotes from them appeared in the next day's *Post* and *Daily News*. "She didn't show any emotion," a twenty-five-year-old juror named Oscarina Aguirre told Bode and a colleague, Dave Goldiner. "That's kind of what did her in." A juror who didn't want her name used told Gorta, "There was nothing believable that she said at all. It just didn't make sense." There had evidently been no disagreement among the jurors. "We all felt she was guilty — we all knew it," Aguirre said. "I don't think anyone thought they didn't do it," the anonymous juror said.

In the first round of voting, however, one juror had written "undecided" on her ballot. I learned of her several months after the verdict, from two young jurors who consented to speak with me on the condition of anonymity. (Five other jurors I reached declined to be interviewed on any terms.) I met with the two separately — I'll call them Tim Smith and Karen Jones — but their accounts were markedly similar. Both reported that the undecided juror had "a personal reason" for her demurral: she was a mother who couldn't bring herself to send another mother to prison and separate her from her child. But, as Smith reported, "we talked to her" and she came around. Smith believed that if Borukhova hadn't testified, the undecided juror — he called her "the Spanish lady" — might have held out longer, if not to the end. He thought that Borukhova's appearance on the stand "put the nail in the coffin." Jones agreed: "She wasn't believable. She would have been better off not testifying." Surely, it didn't matter whether Borukhova testified or not. By the time she took the stand, Leventhal's powerful narrative — outlined in his opening statement and fleshed out by his witnesses — had done its work. It was too late to de-suspend the jurors' disbelief. When Scaring announced that Borukhova would testify, "I saw Brad and Donna chuckling," Smith recalled.

Both jurors called Strauss's decision to change custody "a good decision." His scathing words from the bench — that Scaring had fought so hard to suppress and Leventhal equally hard to admit — seemed entirely reasonable to them. "Why would a judge take such a drastic step if there wasn't a good reason for it?" Jones said. "Why would so many people be against her?" Smith said, "That lawyer for child aid who painted a portrait of her as overbearing. Why would he lie?"

Both accepted the F.B.I. translator's version of the disputed line in Borukhova's taped conversation with Mallayev — "Are you going to make me happy?" — as correct. "Why would he be working for the F.B.I. if he didn't know what he was doing? He had no reason to say something that wasn't true," Jones said and went on to make the inference that Leventhal intended her to make: "She had led Mallayev to believe there would be some other payoff in addition to money. She had given him hope." That the taped conversation took place in May — five months before the murder — did not shake Jones's conviction that it was connected to the crime. "She was sensing that there would be a need to get rid of Daniel," she said. The defense's version — "Are you getting off?" — seemed unworthy of consideration: "They were grasping at straws," Jones said. Smith's imagination, too, had been fired by the idea of sex between Mallayev and Borukhova. "He wouldn't risk his life for $20,000. There must have been something more. A chubby, older man would want a relationship with her, a thin, younger woman." (I asked the thin and young Smith if he found Borukhova attractive, and he gave me an incredulous look. Then he said with a smile, "Slightly below average for me.")

Borukhova's contained, Cordelia-like demeanor at the defense table worked against her. Nothing came of nothing. "She had no emotion," Jones said. "She didn't seem upset. She wasn't scared. If you're innocent and being tried for murder, you'd be upset. They dressed her in white to subliminally signal her innocence. Who wears white every day?" Smith used the words "cold," "detached," "aloof," "stiff," and "unconcerned" to describe Borukhova. Jones thought her "irrational," "unnatural," and "obsessed" as well.

For Jones, the film of the traumatic transfer of custody was conclusive evidence of Borukhova's monstrousness: "She was cold and unconcerned. She didn't try to comfort her daughter. Wouldn't you want the child to be calm? But she just wanted to show on tape how upset the child was. I don't know what her motivation could have been, except selfish. The child fell asleep. Then she had the nerve to wake her up. I saw that she was willing to sacrifice the well-being of her daughter to get her way. This made me believe she would kill her husband to keep the daughter."

Neither juror had much to say about Mallayev. Confident that the weight of evidence was sufficient to convict him, Leventhal had not troubled himself over the chubby hit man's portrait, allowing him to emerge as the characterless instrument of Borukhova's will. Both jurors were sure of Mallayev's guilt, though Smith had noticed—and thought unfair—Hanophy's suppression of Siff's attempt to challenge the fingerprinting field. Jones thought otherwise. "He was trying to say fingerprinting is not a science. That's ridiculous. It was such a crazy argument, such a desperate thing to do. They've been using fingerprinting for so many years. Why would they use it if it wasn't accurate?"

The two jurors also differed in their estimates of the lawyers and the judge. Smith preferred Scaring to Leventhal. "Scaring was convincing right off the bat. He had a presence about him. His height. We were very impressed with him," whereas the short Leventhal "doesn't immediately strike you." Jones preferred Leventhal and was critical of Scaring's cross-examination technique. "He was obvious. You could tell what he wanted the person he was cross-examining to say." Smith said he thought the judge "was slightly biased toward the prosecution. I thought Leventhal got away with showmanship. I was interested that the judge didn't clamp down on him." Jones said, "I thought the judge was impartial," and added: "I liked him a lot. He seemed real and down to earth and serious about his job. And funny. He had a good sense of humor."

Smith described his fellow jurors as "very passive. No A-personalities. Everyone was laid back." He said that some jurors disregarded the judge's edict not to talk about the case during lunch, and that a few jurors had watched the case on the news. One of the jurors who turned me down had written in an e-mail: "I don't think I could do the interview without getting very upset about it. It still feels too recent for me to talk about it." I imagine that she was the Spanish lady on whose thread of maternal feeling Boru-khova's fate briefly hung.

19

THE Queens Supreme Courthouse was built in 1960 and is an example of the civic architecture of the period, whose pointless ugliness age cannot wither, and whose entrance lobby was rendered a complete aesthetic catastrophe by the post-9/11 array of security equipment brutishly installed across its width. I had been coming to the courthouse for several weeks before I noticed the mosaic that covers the space over the entrance leading to the elevators and the adjacent walls. The mosaic is a wondrous sight, but, as people hurry through the security barrier toward the elevators, they do not take it in. I noticed it only because one day, during a long recess, I was walking around the courthouse looking for things to notice.

It is a work of the most extreme complexity and strangeness. Its creator was the artist and sculptor Eugene Francis Savage (1883–1978), who did murals for the W.P.A. and for Yale, Columbia, and Purdue universities, and designed the Bailey Fountain at Grand Army Plaza in Brooklyn. The piece is a sort of mad allegory illustrating concepts —spelled out along its bottom—that relate to a court of law: Correction, Exoneration, Rehabilitation, Security, Plea, Inquiry, Evidence, Error, and Transgression, along with the deadly sins of Vanity, Envy, Hate, Lust, Sloth, Perdition, and Avarice. Over "Correction" stands a grim man with lightning coming out of one wrist; "Avarice" is represented by an ugly old woman wearing a blue dress and pearl necklace and bent over a box of money and jewels. Near the grim man, a small mean-looking fellow crouches at the entrance to a tunnel out of which another unpleasant person, carrying tools, crawls. A hooded figure with arms outstretched, holding a golden tape measure, a naked guy with a bow and arrow, a bare-chested man kneeling near a pile of books on top of which there is a hammer and sickle, a woman with nice breasts, a hideously grimacing black man—these are some of the other figures, set in a sinister landscape crowded with waterwheels and mountains and roads and rainbows and blue bowls filled with gold. The eye doesn't know where to rest. A vertiginously tipped scale of justice hovers over the allegory, one of its golden pans poised high in the air and the other swinging close to the ground. Oddly, the pan poised high in the air holds a book with the word LAW on its cover, while the pan low to the ground holds nothing but a sort of peach pit. Is this a comment on the weightlessness of the law? Or is it just Savage exercising his gravity-defying artist's imagination — secure in the knowledge that the fate of public art is to be invisible to the public that never ordered it?

20

B EYOND the elevators is a glass door leading to an area where the public is not allowed, except with special credentials — here are the offices of the district attorney. On March 18th, I was admitted to this inner sanctum for an interview with Brad Leventhal. Kevin Ryan, the D.A. press officer who had arranged the interview, remained in the conference room where it took place. Leventhal gave me his history: "I was born in Brooklyn. My father was a furrier and salesman and a decorated soldier in World War II. My mom was a stay-at-home mom. I'm an only child." When he was sixteen, Leventhal's parents moved to Long Island, where he went to high school, college (Nassau Community College and C. W. Post Long Island University), and law school (Hofstra). After graduation, he worked as a defense attorney for the Legal Aid Society and then went into private practice, specializing in homicide. After eight years, he left criminal defense and became an assistant D.A. "I just didn't enjoy the work anymore. I didn't feel good about what I was doing. I wasn't getting fulfilled." And no wonder: Leventhal had just defended a doctor named David Benjamin, who had horribly botched an abortion and allowed a patient to bleed to death on a table in his storefront clinic. "After that trial, I was just not interested — I was thinking about getting out of law entirely," Leventhal continued. "But I had always wanted to be a prosecutor, and I had developed a nice relationship with the assistant D.A. who tried the case against me, and I called him up and asked him whether there were any openings here at the D.A.'s office, and about three or four months later I was employed here."

As I questioned Leventhal about the trial he had just won, it was clear that his dislike of and contempt for Borukhova had not been feigned. "She made the decision to lie when she got up on the witness stand," he said severely. "That was *her* choice. No one forced her into giving any particular type of testimony." He went on:

> There are consequences when you don't tell the truth. For instance, what a tremendous lie she told when she said that on August 1, 2007, both Mr. and Mrs. Mallayev came to her office and asked for a prescription for this uncontrolled hypertension she claimed the wife suffered from. And I didn't confront her with it on cross-examination. I knew she would try to come up with some sort of lie. So I left it alone. But in summation I was able to show — through documentation

that was in evidence before she ever testified — that Mallayev was out of the country on August 1, 2007.

I complimented Leventhal on his cleverness. I said I had wondered at the time why he had put a Delta Airlines clerk on the stand to establish that Mallayev had flown to Israel on July 29th and returned to Atlanta on August 20th. "Now I know you were preparing—"

"No, no," Leventhal cut in. "I wasn't. When I put in that evidence, I had no idea she was going to testify."

"Then why did you put it in?"

Leventhal explained that he was accounting for a gap in Mallayev's cell-phone records; he was merely establishing that during his stay in Israel, Mallayev's cell phone was out of use. "Little did I know that she was going to get up on the witness stand and lie."

"She hadn't paid attention to the airline clerk's testimony."

"Or had forgotten. My father always told me 'It's easy to tell the truth. You don't have to have a good memory to tell the truth. You have to have a very good memory if you're going to lie.'" He added, "One of the jury's first notes was to ask for the Delta flight records."

I said, "Perhaps her memory was affected by malnourishment. You've seen the early pictures of her and how she looked at the trial."

"I thought she looked fine," Leventhal said coldly. "Mr. Mallayev trimmed down as well. He looked fine."

"Yes, he looked fine. But I thought she looked pretty unhealthy. You don't think so?"

"I don't think so. I thought she looked pretty good. She looked pretty healthy to me. She was trim. She was well dressed. She was well manicured. And the court staff went out of their way to try and obtain kosher meals for her and fresh fruit, and she refused it. So I think it's of her own creation."

I again mentioned the pictures of a healthy and round-faced Borukhova that appeared in the newspapers at the time of her arrest and the diminished Borukhova of the trial.

"She doesn't look that different to me from the time I met her after she was arrested," Leventhal insisted, and he added: "She's not at a day spa."

At the end of the interview Leventhal treated me and his minder to a Handelesque aria about the delights of working in the D.A.'s office. "From the day I started, until today, there's never been a day—and this is an amazing thing—there's never been a day when I've regretted my decision or said 'what if.' Not a day. I love coming to work. I love doing this job. The people that you work with here are wonderful people. You don't have to worry about representing a client or the interests of a particular client. You don't have to worry about making money and getting paid. You don't do this for the money, that's for sure. All you have to worry about, all you have to focus on, is trying to do justice. And I believe that justice was certainly served in this case."

21

WHEN I spoke with Scaring a few weeks later and mentioned Leventhal's entrapment of Borukhova in her testimony about Mallayev's August 1st visit, he was dismissive: "What did she say in her testimony? She said I saw them on August 1st. She looks in her file and sees the wife was there and uses the plural instead of the singular. It was a slip of the tongue. Or she misremembered. It was a year and a half ago. It made no difference whether he was there or not. It had nothing to do with anything. And Leventhal knew that but was able to parlay it into a significant event. And that troubles me about the jury. This is a murder case. You convict somebody because they said 'them'?" *They said them.* Scaring was repeating the very "slip of the tongue" he attributed to Borukhova — one that has been creeping into the language. There was an exchange in the criminal trial in which this popular solecism comically figured. Michael Anastasiou was questioning a witness named Alex Kryzhanovskiy, who was on 64th Road at the time of the murder and saw a man running up the street. After describing the man's apparel, Kryzhanovskiy said, "Oh, there was also one more thing. They also had a piece of white cloth I believe on the right side of their body that they were holding to their body as they were running." The colloquy continues:

Q: Do you recall the general age of this individual?
A: I remember telling the detective I believe it was somebody

in their thirties. That's the impression they made on me. I think they — I said it was somebody in their thirties.

Anastasiou caught the "they" infection himself: "And what direction were they going in?" and "What did you, if anything, observe them do after they went up the block?" he asked. "They were running on the street," Kryzhanovskiy replied. The dialogue took a farcical turn:

The Court: Are you saying they?
The Witness: The person. The person, I'm sorry. The person was running up the street . . . and then they crossed over on the other side of the street towards — as they got near the intersection on 102nd Street and appeared to make a right turn. I remember saying that as far as I could see they made a right turn on 102nd.
The Court: You keep saying they. You mean —
The Witness: The person, the man.
The Court: The person.
The Witness: I'm sorry.

When I interviewed Scaring early in the trial, he had been as — or almost as — buoyant as Leventhal. He said that the prosecutors had a "lousy case" against Borukhova and that all they could hope for was that Mallayev, against whom they had a stronger case, might pull her down with him. "They had wiretaps out and they weren't able to obtain any incriminating evidence," he said. "They had search warrants all over the place, and they weren't able to get any incriminating evidence. They interrogated Mallayev for hours trying to get him to implicate Borukhova, and he never did," he went on. "We're going to argue that the circumstances are not compelling and that it is clear Daniel had other enemies. Who they are and what motive they may have had nobody ever looked at. The prosecutor only looked at Dr. Borukhova." But Scaring never produced the alternative scenario with other enemies that would have cleared Borukhova, and now he was upset and bitter, the wounded lion, who no longer cares if a journalist hears him whimper.

"You know, defending an innocent client is the hardest thing for a defense lawyer. I didn't take the case until I talked to her at length, and I believed she was innocent from the beginning."

"But who did it if those two didn't? In order to clear the innocent you need to find the guilty."

"It's supposed to be the other way around. You're supposed to be presumed innocent."

"The presumption of innocence is a kind of travesty isn't it?" I said, to see what Scaring would say.

"The prosecution does have an overwhelming advantage," he said. "The jury walks in and figures the defendant wouldn't be there if he wasn't guilty. They don't trust the defense lawyer. And if there is any bias by the judge, if there is any body language by the judge that supports that bias, it becomes almost impossible to overcome." Scaring spoke of Hanophy's bias by body language: "During the prosecution's summation, Hanophy sat behind his desk intently listening. During the defense summations he walked around looking bored."

Scaring, like many criminal defense attorneys, started his

career as a prosecutor. In the first interview, he talked at great length about a case he had tried as a young assistant D.A. in Nassau County—"the most exciting case I ever tried"—against a Dr. Charles Friedgood, who had given his wife a fatal injection and then cut her body into pieces. After he won his conviction of Friedgood, the "routine" murder cases that followed bored Scaring and impelled him toward the defense law he has practiced ever since. Scaring had initiated the investigation of Friedgood and was entirely convinced of his guilt. I asked him if, knowing what he knew, he would have taken the case as a defense attorney. "Sure," Scaring said. "Absolutely. May even have won it." When I asked him what it is like to win an acquittal for someone you know is guilty, he talked about something else. Now I pressed him again on the subject, and again he dodged. "What keeps prosecutors and police detectives on their toes is the knowledge that they're going to confront qualified advocates. It makes the system work better. And I'll leave it at that."

I asked him if he would have done anything differently in his defense of Borukhova.

"What would have happened if I hadn't put her on the stand? I think they would have convicted her in a heartbeat. No, I don't have any regrets. There was nothing I could do about my summation. I had to give it. It would have been nice if I could have stood up on Friday morning and said to the judge: I can't give the summation because I'm not prepared. But as a lawyer I don't have that kind of independence, I have to follow the directions of the court. If I had said, 'I can't give the summation' he could have said, 'You don't give it, you waive it.' I'm an honorable person. I wouldn't call in sick when I'm not sick. There was no option but to proceed unprepared. So she was denied her constitutionally protected right of effective assistance of counsel."

22

ON a Sunday afternoon a few days after the verdict, Alla Lupyan-Grafman took me on a tour of the Bukharan neighborhood in Forest Hills, a district of pleasant houses on side streets that flank an avenue (called 108th Street) lined with well-maintained red brick apartment buildings. After about eight blocks, the avenue becomes shabbier (a few synagogues appear) and then turns into a Main Street stretch of food markets and small clothing and electronics stores and storefront offices, among them the medical office where Borukhova practiced. Before we reached the Annadale playground on 64th Road off Main Street — our final destination — Alla led me through side streets where the McMansions of which she had spoken had risen and were still rising. They were an amazing sight. But it wasn't only their size that made me stare with wonder. With their ornate stone columns and gilded wrought-iron balustrades and balconies, and two-story windows, they looked not like private homes but like embassies. One imagined balls and receptions going on in the rooms within;

one did not imagine families sitting down to dinner or watching TV. Many of these buildings were in a state of half- or near-completion; workmen were coming in and out of them. I asked Alla who the Bukharan immigrants were who could afford such residences and where their money came from. She shrugged and said, "Mafia," but could not elaborate. The word "mafia," like the word "nature," often stands for what can't be known. One morning, Hanophy's courtroom had been riveted by the testimony of a Georgia bank official who testified to the millions of dollars her bank had, incredibly, lent Mallayev for a housing development he was constructing outside of Atlanta, even though it knew that he was hundreds of thousands of dollars in debt to credit-card companies, among other creditors. No explanation was given for the bank's crazy largesse. The forces by which the economy is ruled — and periodically decimated — are not for us to fathom.

Alla and I reached the shopping area and turned onto 64th Road. The Annadale playground was a block and a half away. At the trial, when the prosecution showed charts on which eyewitnesses to the shooting made marks to indicate where they had stood when they saw what they saw, I had had trouble imagining the scene, and now that I was on the spot it was not much clearer. The place was just another of the city's grudging concessions to the claims of innocuous childhood pleasure. No trace of violence appeared among its banal swings and slides. But a block away, a trace of the victim remained. As Alla and I passed a red brick apartment building on 64th Road, she pointed to a red canopy over a white door on which the words "Ortho-dontist / Physical Therapist" were printed. "This was Daniel's office," she said. Disconcertingly, the name of the man who had been dead for seventeen months still appeared on a sign hanging beside the door from a metal pole: "Daniel Malakov, D.D.S. P.C. Orthodontist," with a Russian translation below it, followed by "Gavriel Malakov, P.T. Physical Therapist," also with Cyrillic writing below. Gavriel, Daniel's youngest brother, had shared the office with him and evidently still practiced there.

The following Sunday, I returned to Forest Hills, impelled by an inexplicable urge to retrace the steps I had taken with Alla. When I paused in front of one of the massive houses to make a sketch of it, a workman came out and invited me in. He spoke English with a Russian accent and proudly showed me the elaborate moldings and embossed wallpapers that were being applied to the walls of the large rooms to give them the requisite, slightly tacky look of Imperial Russian splendor. On 64th Road, I took out my notebook again, to write down the words on the sign in front of Daniel's dental office. As I stood writing, a tall, older man in a yarmulke suddenly appeared, whom I immediately recognized as Khaika Malakov. He looked at me without surprise or even interest, as characters in dreams do. I, too, felt no surprise. I introduced myself as a journalist — perhaps he remembered seeing me in the courtroom? — and asked if we could talk. Khaika silently took out a key and opened the white door. I followed him into a waiting room in which everything was black: the high receptionist's counter, the linoleum floor, the chairs in a row along a wall. Khaika motioned me to one of the chairs and seated himself in the next one. "Everybody congratulate me," he said. "You win case. Justice is done. But in this case nobody win. Especially Michelle. I lost my son. My lovely, lovely son. He had high education. Everybody need him. Very high-class specialist, very important. My family lost him. Everybody lost. Nobody win. All the families suffer. Killer family suffer now. This case, it is not sport, it is not business transaction. It is very stupid case. A lot of people congratulate me. I don't know what to say."

Khaika began to speak with great anguish and bitterness of the death of his daughter, Stella, the oldest of his four children, which occurred a year before the murder of his son. She was treated for leukemia at Sloan-Kettering with an experimental drug whose side effects, Khaika believed, killed her. He had tried to intervene—he said he knew that the drug would fatally weaken her immune system—but was rebuffed by the brusque doctor who administered it. Stella died of pneumonia, as Khaika predicted she would, at the age of forty. He hates the doctor.

He spoke of "family who killed my Daniel" and of his certainty that Borukhova's mother and sisters and brother were partners in the plot; he said he would like to see them prosecuted. He proposed that an electrode be placed in Borukhova's brain so that "every time she touched her head she would remember what she did." He went on, "American jail system is not like Russian system. They have TV, they don't work, they can go to school. They can just exercise. Too easy. In Russian jail it is very hard."

I said—falling into Khaika's associative style of conversing—that in *Crime and Punishment* Raskolnikov got only eight years in Siberia.

"Eight years in Siberia is like eighty years here," Khaika said. "It's very cold in Siberia. They work underground in mines. After three years everyone is sick." He returned to the Borukhova family. "Marina lied for three days. The whole family has a bad personality." He said that Natella had five children and had never allowed her husband's parents to come to her house.

I had learned that Ezra Malakov was a distinguished disseminator and performer of *Shash maqam*, a classical Central Asian musical genre, and had made a number of CD recordings. I asked Khaika where I could get one. Khaika said he had a collection of Ezra's recordings at home and invited me to come pick one up. As we walked to his house, we passed an apartment building that Khaika identified as the building where Borukhova's mother and sisters live. On 108th Street, we passed Borukhova's storefront office, and I saw that her sign, like Daniel's, was still in place. Khaika's house, a few blocks away on a side street, is not one of the McMansions; it is a small brick house of pleasant, undistinguished character. The living room had a stilted orderliness. There was a large polished table in the middle surrounded by large chairs, a huge credenza with china and crystal, tea sets, and bibelots behind its glass front, a large painting in a gold frame of the Wailing Wall in Jerusalem, a black upright piano, Persian rugs, leather sofas, and, in the window, a vase of gladiolus and hydrangeas.

Along with the CD, Khaika gave me a book that he had written about Stella entitled *Legend of a Beloved Daughter.* Half the text, illustrated with color photographs, was in Russian, followed by an awkward English translation. In spite of sentences like "Never did she hang out in the dark with a guy," the image of a woman of exceptional physical, intellectual, and moral beauty emerges. Stella seemed to have no flaws. She was modest, generous, spirited, entirely lovable, brilliantly intelligent, and exceptionally good-looking. She was a high school math teacher who was able to bring comprehension even to students who had fallen hopelessly by the wayside in previous math classes; she wouldn't rest until they got it. "Reading this book," Khaika wrote,

> people would think "There, a person passed away, and in order of remembering that person, people try to write up an unrealistic human being." NO, dear reader, she really was real, an extraordinary being. . . . God sent a creation saying: Here, people, look at my creation! Look at what I can create, and if you can, learn from it!! God kept her on earth long enough to have her leave her mark on others, and then took her back.

The songs on Ezra's recording were like no songs I had ever heard. Over instrumentation that, in its circular, teasing rhythms and vibrant twangings, evoked harem dancers, the words *baruch atah adonai* rang out in Ezra's vigorous, harsh voice. After I played the CD a few times, I began to like it.

23

THE sentencing hearing, on April 21st, had the atmosphere of a public execution. The jury box was filled with cameramen, who stood in a row and thrust their heavy cameras outward, as if they were rifles. Every seat was filled. The front row had again been reserved for police detectives and functionaries from the D.A.'s office, and the horde of Malakovs seemed even larger than the one that had come to hear the verdict. Judge Hanophy arrived in a Sunday-best gray suit; he put on his robe only at the end of the obligatory waiting period. Borukhova and Mallayev were led in but not immediately freed from their handcuffs; Scaring had to ask Hanophy that this be done. Borukhova wore a turban of patterned ivory fabric, a long black-and-white skirt, and her white jacket. Mallayev was in a dark suit. Throughout the hearing, Borukhova wrote on a yellow legal pad. Scaring and Siff had submitted motions "to vacate the conviction," and Donna Aldea stood up to give the prosecution's argument against them. As she neatly struck down Scaring's and Siff's complaints of unfairness and bias, I thought of Billy Gorta's admiring characterization of her as head girl at a British school.

After Scaring and Siff had responded in turn, and the judge had said, "Motions are denied," the sentencing hearing proper began, with a series of "victim impact" statements. The first statement was read aloud by Khaika Malakov, in Russian, with Alla translating. He spoke of Daniel's professional merits and personal virtues. He expressed his gratitude to the police and to the D.A.'s office. "We know how difficult it would be to find the killer and how difficult it is especially under democratic system to prove the guilt." He complimented Hanophy on his "professionalism," pausing to remark that, early in the trial, "I thought that the judge was actually leaning toward the defendants, toward the criminals. He seemed to be cruel to me. He didn't let me scream or cry in the courtroom so we were crying in silence and we were screaming inside in this courtroom and we were suffering quietly." He repeated his remark about the emptiness of the congratulations he received after the verdict: "There is no winners here." He concluded by saying "Like it says in the old book, eye for eye, death for death, but fortunately for the killers who commit such a crime there is no such penalty in the United States today." He asked for life imprisonment without parole.

Gavriel made a brief statement (in English) and requested the same sentence. Then Leventhal read letters from Daniel's mother and from a nephew and niece — Stella's children, Yuri Normatov and Lyudmila Normatova. The mother recalled Daniel's birth in the ambulance taking her to the hospital. "I delivered him quickly, gently and easily. Daniel came into this world in this way and lived his life in the same way." Yuri wrote of his uncle as "an individual who wanted to get the most out of his life. He wanted to learn about art and fashion, literature, poetry and music. His goal was to be a cosmopolitan man." He said that Daniel's "last breathing days were the happiest days of his life," and went on,

> I can say that with 100 percent confidence. I remember coming into his office a few days after Michelle was living with him. I remember everything perfectly. Michelle was playing a game with his secretary. Daniel was taking a break. He was sitting in the other room eating a pomegranate. He told me "when I see Michelle playing at school I think back to how much time passed that I wasn't with her and cry."

Of course he was eating a pomegranate. Characters in Russian literature are always eating (or offering) fruit at significant moments. (Gurov in *The Lady and the Lapdog* eats a slice of watermelon after he and Anna have slept together for the first time; Oblonsky in *Anna Karenina* is bringing Dolly a large pear when she confronts him with his infidelity.) It is in the blood of Russian storytelling to take note of the fruit. The image of Daniel's pomegranate briefly flickered in the minds of the people sitting in the Queens courtroom and disappeared until, many months later, it leaped out of the trial transcript that one of the spectators was reading.

The niece wrote that Daniel "always knew that his wife's lies and false allegations were obvious," and that "everyone always confront[ed] him with the question how are you letting Mazoltuv get away with torturing you like this? They all knew that her major goal was to make his life miserable as a revenge for divorcing her."

Then Leventhal made his own statement. The job he loved so much required that he grow emotional and angry. His high voice rising and his hands feverishly gesturing, he called Mallayev a predator and schemer and evil accomplice. He shrilly castigated Borukhova for her "sheer arrogance" in believing that she could get away with the crime and for her violation of the Hippocratic oath (though he continued, insultingly, to call her "Miss" rather than "Dr."—as did the judge) "when she hired a paid assassin to murder in cold blood the man who had once shared her bed." Borukhova listened impassively, and continued to write on her legal pad. Leventhal characterized the crime as "one of the most coldhearted and coldblooded murders that I have had the opportunity to investigate and to prosecute." (Surely *the* most coldhearted and coldblooded case he had prosecuted [also before Hanophy] was the heartless and pointless murder of an eighteen-year-old Chinese delivery boy in February, 2004, by three teenagers who beat and stabbed him to death when he came to the door with food they had ordered from his father's restaurant with the intention of robbing him so that they could buy fashionable sneakers.) He said, "These defendants are a true danger to society," and he asked for the maximum sentence. "It is only these sentences, Your Honor, that will protect society from criminals such as these."

Siff pleaded for the minimum sentence for Mallayev. (As,

thirteen years earlier, Leventhal had pleaded for the abortionist: "Judge, he's no threat. This man brings no danger to society. He's a man who tried to do his job," the *Times* quoted him as saying — doing *his* job at the abortionist's sentencing.) Then Hanophy asked Mallayev if he had anything to say before being sentenced. The man who had sat in silence during the whole trial now rose and spoke at length. He spoke in broken but fairly comprehensible English, in a rambling, confusing, entirely unpersuasive, but strangely dignified way about how he had been railroaded. "I didn't kill nobody in my life," he said, and went on:

> I cannot blame the jury for the verdict because they hear what they have to hear and what they supposed to hear to bring that judgment because Mr. Prosecutor make everything to make that happen. For holding the media, the news channel, all advertisement, and to over and over with lie statements in the newspapers, to putting the media. Is like hey, we got the killer, this is the killer, and make believe to whatever he's talking with no proof.

And:

> What they try to accomplish is to satisfy the people of New York hey we got the killer. Don't worry. You can go to the playground. Nothing is gonna happen.

Mallayev recalled the statement he had made after he was extradited: "From first day of the court when I mention I live by Ten Commandments, Mr. Prosecutor and including Your Honor you both laugh on that." He continued, "But the truth is I feel comfortable for myself and I'm clear in front of myself and in front of God and nobody can make me kill somebody."

Scaring then stood up to argue for a lenient sentence for Borukhova. He said, as he had said to reporters many times before, that the case against her was based on "guesswork and speculation." He said that she, like Daniel, was respected in the community for being a good doctor and a good person. "It's easy for the prosecution to stand up and wave his hands and say this is the worst case he's ever seen, but he doesn't know her, either. She is a good person. I'm asking Your Honor not to impose such a Draconian sentence on this good person."

The Judge said, "Miss Borukhova, do you want to say anything before I sentence you?"

Borukhova made the briefest of statements: "I would just repeat myself again and again as I mentioned at the time when my husband was killed, I had nothing to do with this murder. I didn't kill anybody. I have nothing to do with it. That's all, Your Honor."

Hanophy gave both defendants the maximum sentence of life in prison without parole. He cited two examples of the "overwhelming evidence in this case." One example was the fingerprints on the silencer and the other was the August 1st incident. "The defendant Borukhova was treating him, meaning the defendant, the defendant, Mr. Mallayev, for some ailment on the very day he was in Israel. That's really long-distance work. Long-distance work." He sentenced each defendant in turn:

Mr. Mallayev, you took the twenty thousand pieces of silver to murder Dr. Malakov. You say you're a religious man. There is a man in the New Testament that says: "What does it profit a man if he gain the wealth of the world and suffer the loss of his immortal soul." Greed led you to this downfall and you are going to pay dearly.

That the man in the New Testament does not figure in Mallayev's religion was evidently of no concern to the judge, who was in his element as he delivered the homily. He then turned to Borukhova, and said:

Miss Borukhova, you set out on a journey of revenge because a judge had the temerity to give the custody of your daughter to your estranged husband. Another quote, Confucius this time, said: "A person who sets out on a path of revenge should first dig two graves." Your husband lies in his natural grave, and you are about to enter your eight-by-eight aboveground internment where you will spend the rest of your natural life.

24

THE City of New York Department of Correction does things in style. When I called the department and said I wanted to visit Rikers Island to see the jails where Mallayev and Borukhova had been held, Stephen Morello, Deputy Commissioner for Public Information, sent a car around to take me there. It was a few weeks after the sentencing, and Borukhova and Mallayev were no longer on the island — they had been taken to their respective permanent prisons — but Morello readily acceded to my request to inspect their former quarters. On the way, the driver, Sean Jones, an agreeable young man, with the title assistant deputy warden, conversed easily about the prison island that had been owned by a family named Ryker and sold to the city in 1884 for $180,000. He told me that between eighty-two and eighty-five percent of the inmates were awaiting trial, and that the rest had received sentences of less than a year. He said that Borukhova and Mallayev had been held in "closed custody" — isolation from other prisoners — because theirs was a "high-profile case." He mentioned that economy measures were being taken at the prison — for example, the twelve slices of bread inmates used to receive daily had been reduced to eight. On the island, Morello, a middle-aged man of pleasing urbanity, awaited us in front of one of the island's men's jails. He took me into the building and, accompanied by a guard, brought me to a corridor of ten or so brutally squalid cells. Most of them were unoccupied, and I was allowed to walk into the one the guard identified as Mallayev's. In it was a metal bed frame, a plastic mattress, two rubber boxes, a rubber wash bucket, a toilet and a sink. White paint was peeling off the tile walls, and the floor was half covered with patches of linoleum and half with the black filth that lies beneath linoleum. There was a radiator under a dirty window. In one of the occupied cells, I glimpsed a man lying on the bed with a gray blanket pulled over his body and head. He could have appeared in one of Savage's allegories, as Hopelessness. Another cell offered an even stranger sight: a woman with long red hair. "It's a transgender woman," Morello said. "If they have male genitalia, they're here." Lunch came and was delivered through a slot in the cell door. It was baloney, mashed potatoes, mixed vegetables, lowfat milk, and four slices of whole-wheat bread.

I was shown a grim shower room, with a cracked tile floor, and then taken to the day room. This was a large space with a gray concrete floor, empty except for a windowed booth, partitioned into six enclosures, and a small television set fixed high up near the ceiling and at a great distance from the booth. The place looked like an installation in an avant-garde Chelsea gallery, but in fact it was where closed-custody inmates could watch television, locked into one of the enclosures for an hour at a time. There was a young prisoner in one of the enclosures, sitting quietly in a plastic chair and looking up at the distant screen, which was showing advertisements. I stood and watched with him, waiting for the advertisements to end and the TV program proper to resume. But it never did. I inspected the rusty locks on the doors of the enclosures; one of them contained a toilet filled with urine. (I wondered how the inmates used the toilet if they were locked into their enclosures.) I looked back up at the television set, and it was still showing advertisements, and the young man was still sitting quietly and looking up at them.

Borukhova's jail, in the Rose M. Singer Building, was less brutal and dirty than the men's jail. Rose M. Singer was a

pioneer of prison reform, and the place reflected her benign spirit. The cells had the same punitive bareness — again,
there was only a bedstead, a mattress, rubber boxes, sink,
and toilet — but they were clean, and each was equipped
with a small TV set. The shower was decent. An atmosphere of mild femininity was present in the building. I
wondered whether women's prisons in general were less
vile than men's. I recalled the testimony of a police detective
named Claudia Bartolomei, who had been present during
Borukhova's police interrogation on the day of the murder,
and who twice made a point of saying (once at a pre-trial
hearing and then at the trial itself), "I took her to my bathroom that had toiletries in it" — as opposed to the "much
dirtier" bathroom used by the ordinary run of involuntary
visitors to the 112th Precinct. "She was a doctor," Bartolomei added. A ripely attractive woman of thirty-three, with
long streaked-blond hair and artful makeup, Bartolomei is
the commanding officer of the 112th Precinct. When she
spared Borukhova the dirty bathroom and brought her to
the place of lovely toiletries, was she signaling her solidarity
with a sister who, like her, had risen in a profession dominated by men? Of course, in calling attention to Borukhova's status as a doctor, Bartolomei was breaking ranks
with the prosecution. When doctors are convicted of
crimes, they lose their license to practice; Leventhal's strategy was to act as if this had already happened: he prolep-
tically stripped Borukhova of her professional status. In his
narrative, she was a plain stay-at-home murderess. Bartolomei gave the account of her kindly gesture in response

to Scaring's charge that the interrogation of Borukhova had been improper — that she received no Miranda warning and that for many hours a lawyer who had been sent to the precinct by one of her sisters was deliberately kept out of the interrogation room. The position of the police was that Borukhova had been questioned as a witness rather than as a suspect, and therefore no Miranda warning (or lawyer) was necessary. Bartolomei's gesture was offered to bolster this position — to demonstrate her respect for Borukhova's rights — but what it actually demonstrated was her empathy with Borukhova's fastidiousness. The gesture had nothing to do with Borukhova being a doctor (what would a doctor want with toiletries?) and everything to do with her being a woman. The fastidiousness of women is an idea that runs deep in our collective unconscious. On Rikers Island, the influence of this concept — and of its corollary that men are "much dirtier" — can be studied and pondered.

25

ON Saturday, May 10th, at 6 P.M., I rang the bell of Khaika Malakov's house on 66th Avenue. When he came to the door he was dressed in a white shirt and navy sweatpants and sandals, and he looked as if he had forgotten the appointment we had made a few days earlier. But he motioned me toward a wicker chair in a corner of his front garden and then went back into the house. The garden was a small flagstone square, bordered by beds of plantings, on which a long white plastic table had been set. Khaika reappeared with a folded white cloth. I watched him remove a bunch of wilted mint cuttings from the table, hose it down, and tilt it so the water ran off. Then he partially unfolded the cloth and laid it across one end of the wet table. He motioned for me to pull up my chair and set my tape recorder on the cloth. He sat down opposite me, and, as we began to talk, Ezra Malakov arrived. He was dressed up (as he had not been on the stand), in a gray suit, blue shirt, white silk tie with a black scroll design, and a porkpie hat, which he took off, to reveal a pompadour of gray hair and a yarmulke. He seated himself at the table, and I asked Khaika to tell him that I had admired his recording. Ezra nodded and picked up the Bukharan newspaper he had brought. Khaika intermittently translated our conversation for him. He was worried about a new development: he had heard that Alan Dershowitz and his brother Nathan had taken over the appeal of Borukhova's conviction. "They invite high-class lawyers. Can do something? You think so?" I said that convictions were hard to overturn. "Of course. Especially Robert Hanophy. He's not stupid. He's very professional. They want to find some mistake for him. He couldn't make mistake."

Ezra said something in Bukhori to Khaika, and Khaika said that Ezra was offering to write an account of Daniel's life and marriage for me. He would send it and I could have it translated. I made a counterproposal: why didn't he speak his account into my tape recorder? Ezra agreed and this is what he said (in Alla's translation):

The trouble between Marina and Daniel started when the girl was born. They were both working and somebody had to raise the child. Daniel wanted to hire a babysitter, but Marina said, "No, my mother will raise the child." And Dani said, "But why, we have the money, we have the possibility, so why make Mom work, why make her suffer when we can hire a babysitter?" But Marina said, "No, the baby gonna be only with my mother. I trust only my mother." And the mother had these stupid principles. She started fighting with Daniel: "Don't do this. Don't do that. Don't give this. She's not supposed to have that."

The baby got sick. She had pneumonia. Daniel took the child to the doctor. The doctor was a Bukharan. And the doctor looked at the child and she said the child should be given water. You shouldn't give her milk. So Dani came back home and told his mother-in-law, "The girl is ill, don't give her milk, just give her water." And that woman, Marina's mother, said, "Bastard, do you know how to raise children? I raised five kids. I know how to raise them. How do you know what to do?" Then Marina came home and saw there was a scandal between Daniel and Istat, and that night he was arrested.

Then Dani couldn't take anymore and he applied for divorce, but she didn't want to have a normal divorce on good terms. She didn't want to be divorced. She wanted to stay in control like the sisters. The sisters don't respect their husbands. The husbands are like dogs for them. The husbands are afraid of them. She wanted to keep him under her control and do whatever she wanted. So when Daniel applied for divorce they came up with new lies, and one of them was that he raped his daughter. He was tortured. He never told us what was going on in his family. He was very private about it. And he lost so much weight. He became a skeleton. He forgot about everything in the world. He was completely pushed to the wall.

There was a court order of protection and he was not supposed to see the girl. But eventually it was proved that it wasn't true, and that it was blackmailing and it was all her own doing, and temporary custody was turned over to Daniel. And she and her mother and sisters and brother couldn't take what happened. They thought Daniel and our family bribed the judge and bribed the witnesses. They never admitted their own guilt and when they couldn't get what they wanted they chose to go on this terrible road. They decided to kill him and they thought that would solve the problem. The girl would go back to Marina and Daniel's money would go to her. That was absolutely stupid. They were very near-sighted and during the trial everything was discovered.

Ezra added a coda to his account:

Marina's mother's brother killed his mother-in-law with an axe. It was about forty years ago. Istat, Marina's mother, is a terrible person. All the people in Samarkand knew how she made her husband suffer. She tortured him constantly. His name was Mirel. He was a manager in a supermarket in Samarkand, a very respectable person. Everybody liked him. He died thirty years ago. [He actually died in 1995.] She was very bad. Before he died he told people on the street, "I'd rather die here on the street than with my wife."

26

TOWARD the end of Ezra's monologue, a man, two women, and three little girls came into the garden. They were Joseph Malakov, the elder of Khaika's surviving children; his wife, Nalia, and their children Sharona and Julie; and Nalia's sister-in-law Roza Younatanova and her daughter Adina. The adults sat down at the table and the children flitted about the garden. Joseph is a pharmacist. His name appears in one of Borukhova's court affidavits, in a paragraph accusing Daniel of poisoning her with drugs — obtained from Joseph — that dangerously increased her thyroid level. Leventhal held up this accusation as perhaps the most outlandish of Borukhova's lies. Joseph is a squarely built, darkly handsome man in his early forties. I found him the most sympathetic of the Malakovs. He is the most assimilated. His near-perfect English is colloquial, and his manner is pleasant and natural. He began to talk about an obscure feeling of guilt that he had about Daniel's death and then asked me not to record our conversation because it was the Sabbath.

Nalia, a slender, dark-haired woman of forty-one, talked about the murder without inhibition. "I saw her at the hospital and I attacked her. I knew one hundred percent it was her. I said, 'Stupid, stupid girl, what did you do? You'll never see Michelle again.'" Nalia, who manages a bridal shop on Queens Boulevard, wore a long skirt but looked like an American woman who has chosen to wear a long skirt, rather than like a Bukharan in her obligatory religious garb. As she talked, I became aware — as one becomes aware of the twittering of sparrows — of soft children's voices. The little girls were hovering around my chair, and one of them, seven-year-old Sharona, was talking about another child. "She is so joyful," she said. "She is always playing." My half-listening turned to full listening when I realized that she was talking about Michelle and wanted me to hear what she was saying. Michelle now lived with Gavriel Malakov and was often at Joseph's house. I asked Sharona, "What do you mean, she is always playing?" and the child explained that Michelle would go on with games long after the other children had tired of them. She was tireless. And "so joyful," Sharona kept repeating. Sharona was a wiry, vivacious little kid, with dancing dark eyes. She was a messenger from the world of children who was trusting me — a stranger from a distant grown-up world — to decode the message of her orphaned cousin's "joy."

I said my goodbyes and left Khaika's garden. As I walked toward 108th Street, I met Gavriel, a lanky young man whose bright-colored clothes had an air of costume, wheeling a stroller with a boy in it and his wife, Zlata, a thin, very young-looking woman with gold-rimmed glasses, holding a baby. A child on a tricycle, peddling vigorously and laughing in a forced and exaggerated manner, preceded them. It was Michelle. Gavriel recognized me from the courtroom and paused to exchange a few words. Walking to the subway I swore at myself. Had I stayed in Khaika's garden another minute, I would have had the chance to observe Michelle in the heart of her feared father's family. But perhaps my glimpse of her face distorted by mirthless laughter sufficed for my journalist's purpose. I thought I got the message.

27

EIGHT days later, on a Sunday evening, I called on Joseph and Nalia at their large (but not oversize) brick house, on tree-lined 68th Road. We sat talking at a table in the spacious, modern kitchen, looking out on a garden with a large blue swimming pool in the middle of it, as their four children — Sharona, six-year-old Julie, fifteen-year-old Simona, and seventeen-year-old Ariel — came in and out of the room, and then disappeared upstairs. The couple offered fruit and tea in small glasses and scenes from the marriage of Daniel and Marina. Joseph said, "When they first got married, they would walk on 108th Street hand in hand. My friends would say, 'What's the matter with them? They're not young kids. Why do they walk hand in hand?' I said, 'Listen, they're happy, who cares?' "

"We don't show affection outside," Nalia said. "We show it inside. It's not customary to show it outside." She went on, "He was very romantic. After weddings, we do *sheva brachot* for the girls, we do parties where people daven for you and wish you happiness. And every night Daniel would make a speech about how he loved her and how she was the woman of his dreams. And it was not appropriate. We do not speak about love. But he would say whatever was in his mind, without thinking what people will say. If I made a speech, I would always have the consideration that I have to say something appropriate to the society."

Joseph and Nalia evidently felt no impropriety in speaking unguardedly to a journalist. Murder violates the social contract, and makes a mockery of privacy. As they had eagerly cooperated with the prosecution, so they eagerly told me their stories — as they had been telling them to other journalists — in the perhaps not so far-fetched belief that journalists are part of the criminal-justice system: small but necessary cogs in its machinery of retribution. As losing defense lawyers are wont to do, Scaring had spoken bitterly of the role of the press in his defeat. He said that the defendants had been tried and convicted in the press, and it is true that the press had made the prosecution's narrative its own. Journalism is an enterprise of reassurance. We do not wring our hands and rend our clothes over the senseless crimes and disasters that give us our subject. We explain and blame. We are connoisseurs of certainty. "Hey, we got the killer. Don't worry. You can go to the playground. Nothing is gonna happen."

Joseph now said, "My niece, Stella's daughter, once asked my brother about husbands and wives. 'What does it mean to be husband and wife?' Daniel took an apple and said, 'You see? This is husband and wife — one thing. No beginning, no end.'" As he told this story (I felt I had heard it before — Khalil Gibran?), Joseph himself took a small beautiful apple from a compote on the table and rotated it in his upheld hand. He went on, "Before the child was born, when Daniel and Marina were first married, he gave himself utterly. When she was in residency in Brooklyn, he would be in his office in Queens accepting patients, and all of a sudden she calls and says 'Daniel, I'm hungry, can you bring me something?' I was there once when this happened. He has an office full of patients. But he leaves, gets her a kosher meal, drives all the way to Brooklyn, gives her the food, comes all the way back. The patients waited for two hours. I said, 'Dani, that's not right.' He said, 'Listen, it's not your business. It's my life, I do it.' He would never draw the line and say stop, it's too much you're asking of me. Whatever she said, it was done. Whether it was reasonable or not, at that point everything was beautiful. Then Michelle was born and now the problems start."

Joseph told another version of the story about the withholding of milk from the baby. "The baby is crying and Daniel tells them that they are feeding the baby improperly. But he's not a pediatrician, he doesn't take that upon himself. He says, let's go to the doctor. So they go to the doctor, the doctor examines the baby, and gives them directions what they have to do: eliminate the food they're giving and give water on a schedule. So he's there, the wife is there, the mother-in-law is there. Everybody hears what the doctor's recommendations are. They come home and they go back to the same way they were doing before. Now Daniel turns around and says, 'Guys. We just went to the doctor. Okay, you didn't take my word. But the doctor gave specific instructions.' So now they say, 'You know what, you shut up.'

I don't know the exact words, but they disregard whatever he says. Now he starts waking up. He starts seeing that the demands are unreasonable." Joseph's cell phone rang and he left the table to talk to the caller.

I asked Nalia about her relationship with Borukhova. "As sisters-in-law we never socialized," Nalia said. She recalled an unpleasant visit to Marina and Daniel's apartment shortly after Michelle was born. "I came with the kids to see the baby, and the mother-in-law didn't let us see the baby. She wouldn't let my kids near the baby. She was like 'get away' to my kids. I was like 'if you don't want my kids next to your baby, I'm not going to send them.' So I never had any contact after that one time."

Joseph came back to the table and talked about the extraordinary ease with which Daniel went through life. "He emigrated after I did and lived with us at first. I already knew what should be done, but still a lot of times things don't work. With him everything was just so nice and easy. He went, got all the paperwork done, everything worked out. He went to York College, then to N.Y.U. and to Columbia for orthodontiary. He did well everywhere."

Nalia said, "I never felt he was in my way. I was pregnant with my son. I said to him, 'I can't clean up after everybody. If you're going to eat, clean up after yourself.' He would say, 'Yes, boss.' He would clean up after himself. He would do his laundry."

Joseph recalled a trip to London with Daniel, Nalia, and Stella. They arrived at the Globe Theatre to see *Much Ado about Nothing*, but it was sold out. Daniel disappeared for a few minutes and returned with tickets he had somehow acquired. Joseph's phone rang again. After he hung up, he said that he had to leave — to get a drug from his pharmacy for a sick relative.

Nalia refilled my glass and said, "We had a thirty-fifth birthday party for my husband. Daniel and Marina came, and when the dancing started everyone was staring at them. She had long hair and she was dancing provocatively. She had one leg on top of his, and she would twist her head so her hair was all over him, and he's bending her down and she's doing all those hand movements. It wasn't a dance you would do in front of people. You could do it in a bedroom or in a night club in Manhattan. You just don't dance like that here. It wasn't appropriate. If I showed you the video — I have it — you'd be shocked." She said that she would look for the video.

Ariel, who had reappeared and was listening to the conversation from the doorway, put Nalia in mind of another of Borukhova's indecencies: "At the birthday party, my son is walking around asking people to make speeches for my husband. When he asks Marina, she just looks at him. She doesn't respect my son. She doesn't say no, I can't make it now, I'll make it later. She just ignores him and turns away."

Ariel said from the doorway, "At her wedding she was wearing this dark-purple lipstick."

"Yes, and she was wearing a black bra underneath the white dress," Nalia said. She paused and added, "Also, she had her period. Either Stella or Joseph told me that they're not going to be together that night. I thought, How stupid can you get? You're never supposed to have your period on the day of the huppah. You go to the doctor and get pills so you don't get your period. You're pure. You're clean. I was like how stupid is this girl. I mean, she's a religious girl. And when she wore the black bra."

"This girl is weird," Ariel said.

"For three dollars you can get a bra," Nalia said.

I invited Ariel to join us at the table, and he came over and sat in his father's place. Ariel spoke admiringly of the house Daniel bought after he moved out of the apartment he shared with Borukhova. "He had a big backyard, grass and trees everywhere. And inside — it wasn't like the house of a billionaire. He made it very simple, elegant, humble, nice. A nice couch, a nice piano, a guitar sitting over there, nice curtains. He knew how to dress. Like his closet. We were at his house after the funeral. We went into his closet. When he was around us in the neighborhood, he always dressed simply, like Marshalls or Sears kind of clothing. But when you went inside his closet, you saw that he had Prada, Armani, Hugo Boss, all those designers. I'm guessing he used to wear that out on dates and stuff like that." I thought, Dr. Jekyll in his Sears khakis and Mr. Hyde in his Armani? And, How does this boy from a religious home and a closed immigrant community know from Prada and Hugo Boss?

"Daniel could get a date like that," Nalia said. "When we were in Europe with him he would be out all night with a different woman."

The mother and son began to talk about Daniel's preoccupation with diet and nutrition. While living with Boru-khova, he had developed stomach pains for which no cause could be found but which prevented him from eating normally and resulted in a great weight loss. "When he separated from Marina, it all sort of went away," Nalia said. But he stayed on his special diet, and remained bone-thin. "The only thing I ever saw him eat was oatmeal or organic rice," Ariel said. Nalia described a meal at her house on the Saturday night before the murder. "Daniel brought Michelle here to eat. I made some soup with macaroni and buckwheat. Daniel wouldn't let her eat the macaroni. He was obsessed with her weight. She was a little chubby child, and he was like 'Make sure you don't give her anything that's fattening.' I'm like 'She's a child. Let her eat. She'll burn it off.' He said, 'No. It's fattening.' So he kept taking the macaroni out. 'Okay. Let her eat the buckwheat. It's healthy.' He was very nutrition- and health-conscious. Brown rice, no white rice, no white flour. He wouldn't let his mother cook anything for him. He would never eat in my house. He would watch what he eats. He was very slim. He would run in the park every day. And that Saturday night when his daughter was here and I gave her soup, he kept taking the macaroni out."

Joseph came back from his errand of mercy and took his seat at the table as Ariel slipped away. Nalia produced a supper of dishes left over from the Sabbath: a fish casserole, an eggplant dish, beets, salad, cheeses, breads. As we ate, she talked about her anxiety after the Strauss decision. "I called Daniel and said, 'You have to give her the baby. You know she's not a normal person. She's very obsessive over

the child. When I'm away from my children for two days —
and I'm a normal person — I go crazy. I call them every day.
She's not a normal person. You have to give her the baby.'
He said, 'Of course I'm going to give her the baby. I never
wanted to take the baby away from her. I didn't know they
were going to give me the child. I'm going to give her the
child. I only want to see the child once or twice a week.
That's it. I don't need custody.' "

Nalia returned to the transgressive dance at the birthday
party. "If I showed you the dance they did, it was like the two
of them were alone in the room. As if they put a perimeter
around themselves, the two of them alone dancing this exo-
tic dance. Stella said, 'If she dances like that, she understands
him. They are meant for each other.' Stella tried to bring
them back together. At first, I, too, thought they were well
matched. They talked about Dostoyevsky and Nabokov and
all these Russian authors. She used to quote from a book
they were both reading. I came once and the two of them
were discussing this book." She turned to Joseph, "Who was
it they were reading when we went to their house?"

"Pushkin?" Joseph said.

"Not Pushkin. Tolstoy. They were reading *Anna Katerina*."

"*Anna Karenina*?" I asked.

"Yes. She was reading that."

"Have you read it?"

"No. I don't like anything with dramas, wars, affairs,
cheating husbands. I like happy endings." I asked her what
she liked to read, and she said the novels of Nora Roberts.

"There's drama in Nora Roberts, but it's light," Joseph

said. He allowed, with a touch of irony, that on Nalia's recommendation he had read a Roberts novel.

"Yes, it's light," Nalia said.

Walking me to the subway, Joseph and Nalia made a small detour to point out Daniel's house, a tall, stately brick house, now rented. I thought of him living there alone, like Rochester. Nalia recalled that on the Friday before the murder Daniel had telephoned to ask her to come over and give Michelle a shower. "I couldn't come because I had to cook for my family. So he got Zlata to come." She went on, "Michelle was with us for a few days after the murder, and I tried to give her a shower, but she wouldn't let me. She wouldn't go into the water. She was crying hysterically, as if we're going to beat her and hit her. She's like 'No, no, no, I'm not going into the shower, no way.' Zlata said it was torture for her to shower her. My theory is that Marina told her 'Never get undressed.' You know she accused him of sexually molesting the child."

"And you feel he couldn't possibly have done that?"

"He used to watch my kids. I trusted him one hundred percent," Nalia said.

We reached the subway and I asked Nalia if she would mail me the video of the dance when she found it. She promised she would.

28

"IF I could just ask you first — how do I learn to like read-ing?" Gavriel Malakov said, glancing at but not taking a book on Chekhov that I was holding out to him. We were sitting in the waiting room of the office on 64th Road, where I had come to interview him.

"You're not a reader?" I said.

"Unfortunately, I'm not. I wish you would teach me to like reading."

"What about reading in your own language?" He shook his head. "You don't like reading in your own language, either?"

"Chekhov! He means so much to me, and yet I never opened any of his books."

"Was school difficult for you?"

"It was a torture camp."

He talked about the marriage of Marina and Daniel in the way the other Malakovs had — about the couple's happiness before the child was born and the unhappiness that fol-lowed. He told some of the same stories, but again, with variations. For example, in his version of the lunch story, Marina would drive from Brooklyn to bring Daniel his mid-day meal as often as he would drive to Brooklyn to bring her hers. What was this about? What erotic ritual were Daniel and Marina enacting as they sped along the Brooklyn-Queens Expressway bearing their beloved's kosher lunch? I would like to ask Borukhova, but I can't. Nathan Dershowitz, who is doing the actual work of the appeal, does not want her to speak to journalists before there is a ruling. She is in the Bedford Hills maximum-security prison for women and "adjusting well," Dershowitz says. Michelle (who continues to live with Gavriel) visits her once a month.

On September 16th, Borukhova was brought to a hearing in Family Court presided over by Linda Tally, who characterized her as an "abusive parent" and granted David Schnall's request that Michelle's visits to her maternal relatives be reduced from three a month to two. Sofya and Istat, as well as Khaika and Gavriel, were in attendance. Schnall, who had grown a scant beard, said he had visited Michelle twice and found that "she's adjusted fabulously." However, he said, after she visits with her maternal aunts and grandmother, she "acts out" and "expresses confusion about where her home is and where it is going to be." Therefore, he argued, there should be fewer visits. Florence Fass vigorously protested, but Schnall prevailed.

During our meeting in April, Fass had described Michelle's visits with her maternal aunts and cousins in heartbreaking detail: "The little girl doesn't want to leave. She's hugging and kissing them. 'Take me home,' she says. She uses excuses to come back. 'I forgot my coat, I forgot my book, I forgot this, I forgot that.' " She added, "My mission is to reunite Michelle with her mother's family — the family she grew up with." But now Fass told the judge that her representation of Borukhova was at an end — Borukhova's money had run out — and she requested court-appointed counsel for her client.

Schnall, astonishingly, objected. His spite toward Borukhova knows no bounds. He said that she owned property
and therefore was not entitled to counsel at taxpayers' expense. Tally turned to Borukhova, who was wearing her
turban and looking thin and gray, and asked if she owned
property. Borukhova said no. Gavriel and Khaika said
something to Schnall, who triumphantly announced that
Borukhova owns a co-op apartment. The judge again questioned Borukhova, and Borukhova tearfully confirmed that
she does. The judge asked Schnall if he wanted a hearing on
the matter, and Schnall said no. The judge picked up a
phone, and, in a few minutes, a gray-haired, heavyset man,
with an irked expression on his face, shambled into the
courtroom, wheeling a lawyer's suitcase. Tally named him
Borukhova's lawyer and set a date for the next hearing, at
which the process of permanently stripping Borukhova of
custody of Michelle would reach its next stage.

29

As fall turned into winter, Borukhova no longer came
to the Family Court hearings but participated in the
proceedings by means of two-way video transmission between prison and courthouse. She appeared in the courtroom on a monitor, a small figure sitting at a table, wearing
a white blouse and a black jumper and a red skullcap. Linda
Tally could speak to her, and she could be heard speaking

back. Tally is a younger judge, with stylishly cut chestnut hair, who speaks in an unmodulated voice and has an impatient, irritated manner, as if her time were perpetually being wasted. Nothing seems to surprise or even interest her. At a hearing on January 12, 2010, Borukhova's court-appointed lawyer, John W. Casey, introduced what might seem a startling subject—"It has been brought to my client's attention that there were marks on the child's face from pinching. We're very happy to hear that the foster father is now agreeing not to do that." Tally responded tonelessly, saying, "That was addressed in the written report. It was stated that basically the uncle, the foster parent, was pinching the child's cheeks, as he claims he does with his other children, as a form of affection. He has been told to stop that and he said he would stop that." To Gavriel, sitting in a back row, she said, "Obviously, sir, not a good idea, because you see what's going to happen, so you're going to stop that, I assume."

When I heard the words "form of affection" and "he said he would stop that" something stirred in my memory (it may be stirring in the reader's as well): I recalled the court paper in which Borukhova, complaining of Daniel Malakov's molestation of Michelle, wrote that "he told me it was his way of showing affection, and promised never to do it again." Is an excess of zeal in expressing affection a Malakov family foible?

Casey then spoke of another injury to Michelle: "There is a very apparent bruise on the child's neck, and we would like to know something about that." The lawyer for the

Administration for Children's Services, which now over-sees Michelle's state wardship, hastened to explain that the bruise was the result of a fall at school. Casey said, "These marks don't look like a fall." At the next hearing, on March 9th, Casey returned to the bruise and said that his client "felt that this was being done in the care of the foster fa-ther," and that "we are beside ourselves, we believe that this child is in danger and in a neglectful home." Schnall re-torted, "Your Honor, the mother continues to make allega-tions that are unfounded, scandalous, and prejudicial." He referred Tally to a school report. According to the report, Michelle bruised her neck when she fell forward against a teacher's desk while rocking back and forth in her chair. Tally accepted the school's explanation and told Casey, "If you have some evidence otherwise, feel free to present that in a legal forum." Schnall once again objected to Boru-khova's having "assigned counsel at public expense, not-withstanding the fact that she's retained Alan Dershowitz. I don't believe he works pro bono." Tally wearily said, "Mr. Schnall, if you think that Mr. Casey should be removed from representing the mother, and we should have her come in and we should have a counsel report and go through the whole process of having her finances looked into and delay this procedure in order to see if she qualifies for an attorney or whether she should retain an attorney, you may file a motion on behalf of that."

In the corridor after the hearing, Khaika, Gavriel, and Joseph exchanged embraces with Schnall as they had with Leventhal at the criminal trial; Natella, Sofya, and Istat sat on a bench, enclosed in characteristic stiff self-containment. But, to my astonishment, when I greeted them, they did not nod and coldly look away. They beckoned to me and asked me to make public their fear that Michelle was being abused by Gavriel. They showed me three color photographs of Michelle with an angry red lesion on her neck. The pictures had been taken, Sofya told me, during a visit with Michelle. "Did Michelle tell you what happened?" I asked. With tears in her eyes, Natella replied, "No. We're not allowed to ask her questions." "What do you mean you're not allowed to ask her questions?" Natella said that the visits are supervised by A.C.S. and that they are prohibited from questioning the child. She handed me the photographs. The mother shook her head and said something in Bukhori to her daughters. "She doesn't want you to have the pictures," Sofya said. I started to hand them back, but the daughters overruled the mother and told me to keep the pictures. Natella said that the Malakovs talk to Michelle about the murder — they tell her that her mother murdered her father. She said that during their visits with Michelle she goes under their long skirts and asks if she can go home with them. She gave me letters from a lawyer and a doctor contesting the school report of a fall, saying the injury could not have been caused by a fall against a table with rounded edges.

At home, I looked at the photographs again. Michelle's wound was glaringly red and severe. Were the sisters' suspicions true? Had someone inflicted it on her? Was she in danger in Gavriel's house? I called the A.C.S. and told the communications director, Sharman Stein, that I had seen disturbing pictures of Michelle Malakov's neck injury. Had the agency seen them? Stein said she had heard about the cheek pinching, but didn't know about the neck injury. She said that she would "look into it" and would call me, observing, "This sounds like angry maternal relatives." She didn't call. Sofya sent an e-mail emotionally reiterating her fears, and enclosing transcripts of the Family Court hearings at which the allegations were rehearsed. But then she stopped replying to my e-mails and phone messages. The sisters had evidently thought better of their impulse to trust a journalist and had retreated to their safe house of stony reticence.

When I called Joseph Malakov and asked to meet with him and his brother and father, he agreed with his usual readiness. On a warm April evening, after a week's delay, because of Passover, I arrived at the house on 68th Road. Only Nalia and the children were at home. As Nalia put plates of savory fried potatoes on the kitchen table in front of Sharona and Julie, she said musingly (and a little artificially, I thought), "I often think of Marina. If she hadn't committed the murder, she would have been with us at the Seder." This led to the subject of Michelle's monthly visits to her mother in prison, which apparently always made the child ill. After the most recent visit, she had been sent home from school with a fever and wasn't well enough to sit at the Seder table; she lay on a sofa in an adjacent room. The little girls excitedly joined in the conversation, relishing the narrative of the child who returns from a visit to her mother in jail and vomits and becomes feverish. They liked saying "in jail."

Khaika and his wife, Malka, arrived and then Joseph, and, finally, Gavriel. Khaika sat next to me at the table, and Malka opposite. Gavriel was on my other side, and Joseph was at the far end of the table, with Nalia in the middle; the little girls hovered near my chair. During my first visit to this house, Joseph and Nalia and Ariel had addressed their remarks to me in turn; but now the family members talked among themselves, in Russian and Bukhori, arguing, interrupting, aware of me, wanting to talk to me, but unable to extricate themselves from their accustomed roles in the family psychodrama. I looked over at Malka, a round, gray-haired woman with a good-natured expression, and asked if she spoke English. She said, "Yes," and added, motioning toward Khaika, "He talks. This is my problem."

Khaika was saying, incoherently, "We need some article to newspaper or to journal about Borukhova family just Marina in the jail. The rest of family going, laughing, lying, and continue life. For me and for my family it is very very"—here he reverted to Russian and Nalia translated: "He is saying he wants to know if you can make an article where Natella and Sofya are responsible for the murder of Daniel. Only Marina is sitting in jail. Why are they walking free? The other two pushed her to do this. They have to be punished for what they did."

I said, "You need evidence of this."

"We have!" Khaika said. He pointed to the inference in Leventhal's closing statement that a sister had been at the playground at the time of the murder.

I said that I would not be able to write the article.

Nalia told the little girls to go upstairs to bed, but as they started to leave Gavriel protested. "Let them stay," he said. "Let them see journalistic excellence at work. Even though they are young and should go to sleep, this is an experience they should not miss." What I took to be Gavriel's elaborate Slavic irony, Nalia heard as serious avuncular advice, and she allowed the girls to stay.

I cut to the chase. "About those allegations," I said.

"Which allegation?" Khaika said.

"The bruise on Michelle's neck." I had the inflammatory photographs in my handbag, but I did not take them out.

Joseph said, "She fell down at school. She goes to a Jewish yeshiva private school. The teachers reported it and described exactly what happened."

I said, "The sisters say she didn't fall. They are afraid she is not safe in Gavriel's house."

"They were afraid Daniel was a pedophile," Joseph lashed out. "They were afraid my mother beat the child. This has been proven a hundred times wrong and wrong and wrong. It's an absolutely ridiculous statement, okay? There is no basis anywhere. We're not child abusers. We don't have to prove to anybody."

"The child was swimming in our pool —" Nalia began.

"That was an innocent accident," Joseph cut in. "Michelle was swimming and another child grabbed her. And they made a big stink that she almost drowned here."

"That we tried to drown her," Nalia said.

"But, Joseph, you jumped in and saved her," I said, remembering from my previous visit Joseph's account of the near-drowning.

"It is devastatingly painful to hear how people who are convicted murderers still have the guts to make allegations," Joseph said.

Julie, now seven, was leaning against my chair, and when I put my arm around her, she molded herself comfortably to me. Julie was a soft, placid child, a different type from the wiry, eager Sharona, but now less shy than she had been a year earlier. Joseph and Nalia's agreeable children reflected their kindly firmness; the household had a sense of ease as well as of order and prosperity. The idea that Joseph was a child abuser indeed seemed ridiculous. But—though Joseph took it as an accusation against the whole Malakov family—the charge of abuse was directed at his brother. I turned to Gavriel and asked him about the cheek pinching.

He replied, "Mazoltuv examines the child on every visit to try to find anything and everything that she can blame us for. So when she saw there was nothing she said, 'I'll just say that they pinched the cheeks.' Because when I personally found out about the allegations, I asked the OHEL representative, 'Did you see anything on the cheek?' and they said 'No, but the mom claimed there was something pinkish.'" (OHEL is a social service agency to which A.C.S. assigns the Orthodox Jewish families under its jurisdiction.)

I said, "In the Family Court, the judge read a report that said you pinched her cheeks out of affection and promised you wouldn't do it anymore."

"I always do like this," Gavriel said and made the gesture of kissing his forefinger and lightly touching my cheek with it. "It is a tradition. It has no physical counterpart."

"Why did you say you wouldn't do it anymore?"

"Because OHEL said, 'From now on we don't want you to show your affection for the child this way.' I said, 'Okay. It will be the way you want.'"

Joseph said irately, "Each and every move you make the other side tries to find something bad. It's not child abuse, God forbid. He said, 'Yes, I did it from affection.' It's not a complicated issue."

I asked Gavriel about another of Casey's accusations at the Family Court: that he had stopped taking Michelle to the therapy the court had mandated.

"Yes, we did not take her consistently to therapy. The therapist was quite aggressive. He told her that your mom killed your father."

"The therapist said that to her?"

"He used this approach. We had difficulty agreeing."

Nalia said, "We never talked about it. She found out from the therapist."

Gavriel said, "He connected her misbehavior and her, let's say, oppositional behavior to the fact that there are hidden emotions. There is a lot of stuff in her that makes her troubled and worried. In order to eliminate that worry, he wanted to confront her with reality so she could help herself get out of it and start on the path to recovery."

"Who was this therapist?" I asked, as if it mattered.

"He's here on Main Street. Richard Meisel. He's a social worker."

At the March 9th Family Court hearing, Sofya, through a personally hired lawyer, had submitted an application for custody of Michelle. The Malakovs now expressed their outrage at the idea of Michelle going to the "killer family."

"But this is the family Michelle knew all her life," I said. "She didn't know your family."

"That's because Marina wouldn't let her come to us."

Joseph said, "It's very simple. It's natural. It's our brother's child. I think any normal human being would feel to have what belongs to you. Why would it even be a question? It's our brother's child."

"This is first of all," Khaika said. "And second, she has to grow up normal, not abnormal. She has to grow up in a normal, reasonable family. The Borukhova family is not normal. It's abnormal. They destroyed everything. Why does she have to go over there again?" He added, "Natella has five children and never has one of the five children gone to the father's mother. Is normal? What do you think?"

"What about Michelle herself? What does she want?" I said.

The family looked at me blankly. Then they began speaking Russian.

I turned to the little girls. "What do you think Michelle wants?"

Sharona thought for a moment. "She really loves my dad," she said.

I asked Gavriel about the bruise on Michelle's neck.

"The bruise was bad. The fall was very bad," he said. "She scratched her neck quite badly. It happened in a class. They were going from Hebrew class to English class. She stood up from the chair. Somebody was walking by and she tripped and the way she fell she fell with her neck on the chair."

If this were a trial, the prosecutor would pounce on the inconsistency between Gavriel's account and the Family Court report in which the child rocked back and forth in her chair. Gavriel's "credibility" would be put in doubt by the disparity. But this was not a trial and I did not think Gavriel was lying. In life, no story is told exactly the same way twice. As the damp clay of actuality passes from hand to hand, it assumes different artful shapes. We expect it to. Only in trials is making it pretty equated with making it up.

Nalia said, "I have to tell you something. Recently, I was in shul and I saw Sofya there and I said, 'What are you doing in the synagogue? Why do you come to prayers here? You shouldn't be showing your face around here. Go to another synagogue.' And do you know what she said to me? She said, 'Do you want to be next?' "

As I was leaving, Nalia apologized for not sending the video of Borukhova's scandalous dance. She explained that Brad Leventhal had asked her not to do so, because of the pending appeal.

30

I N the fall of 1992, an N.Y.U. law professor named Martin Guggenheim was approached by an eleven-year-old boy who was the object of a custody battle and had been assigned a law guardian he despised. In an article entitled "A Law Guardian by Any Other Name: A Critique of the Report of the Matrimonial Commission" (2007), Guggenheim wrote, "The child told me that although he thought his lawyer would be someone fighting for what he wanted, he came to regard his lawyer as his enemy because the law guardian consistently sought things the child did not want. The child asked me to represent him." Guggenheim took the case and succeeded in ridding the boy of the loathed law guardian. The case was reported in the *Times* — "11-Year-Old in Custody Battle Wants to Trade in His Lawyer" and "Boy in Divorce Suit Wins Right to Choose His Lawyer" — and brought other aggrieved children to Guggenheim's door. Guggenheim writes:

> They all told me that they wanted a lawyer who would fight for them. After I explained to them that the law guardian is

not obliged to seek the outcome the child wants, the children made clear that, if they could not have a lawyer who would seek what they want, they would much prefer not having a lawyer at all. . . . Children, at least those I have met, dislike hypocrisy most of all. They can comfortably accept not being permitted an attorney. But they deeply resent being assigned someone who calls herself an attorney and then behaves inconsistently with the core meaning of what attorneys are.

Guggenheim is an authority in a field that he entered in the 1970s — the beneficent new specialty of children's rights — which he gradually came to regard as a kind of mockery of itself. In his book *What's Wrong with Children's Rights* (2005), he argues that the concept of children's rights is actually a disguise for adults' desires, "a mantra invoked by adults to help them in their own fights with other adults." And he sees the law guardian as a particularly noxious outgrowth of the "best interests of the child" doctrine, through which the interests of embattled adults are advanced in the courts. In "A Law Guardian by Any Other Name," Guggenheim reports that, after the case of the eleven-year-old boy, he never again succeeded in persuading a judge to remove a law guardian whose child-client felt betrayed. He came to see "the degree to which judges regard law guardians as court aides, not as children's lawyers." One judge told him, "The only client the law guardian had, I thought, was me," and went on to explain, "The law guardian serves at the Court's pleasure, not at the pleasure of the [child]." Another judge said that she "wanted a law guardian to help her decide the case. She was very pleased with the law guardian's performance. The children's feelings on the subject simply were irrelevant."

When I spoke with Guggenheim about the Sidney Strauss decision, he sighed and said, "The story is so familiar to me." About Schnall he shrugged and said, "He was not entrusted with any task except to do what he wanted." Lawyers for children, he went on, "know no boundaries — because there are no boundaries." Unlike a lawyer for an adult, who is required to put his client's wishes before his own, the lawyer for a child labors under no such constraint. Under cover of the "best interests of the child" doctrine, his own inclinations predominate. In *What's Wrong with Children's Rights,* Guggenheim writes,

> Time and again I have seen lawyers choosing for themselves what outcome to argue for on behalf of their child clients and gaining the advantage in the case for no other reason than that they became the recognized voice for the children's interests. Even when the judge knows full well that the position the children's lawyer is taking is really nothing more than the product of the lawyer's personal views, judges give considerable weight to that lawyer's position.

He continues:

> I have been involved in countless cases in which young children were represented by counsel. The one constant through these cases is the crucial need for the parent's attorney to win the support of the child's attorney to maximize the chances for success. This does not mean the child's lawyer's view

always controls. But it is vitally important because it often can be devastating to a party's hopes for success if the child's lawyer proves to be a foe.

On March 1, 2010, Casey filed a motion in Family Court, on Borukhova's behalf, asking for Schnall's disqualification and removal as Michelle's law guardian, on the grounds that he was a witness at the criminal trial, and that he was biased; but at the March 9th hearing — consistent with Guggenheim's experience — Tally bluntly refused to relinquish her court aide. She had no illusions about Schnall: in the 2007 Family Court proceeding she often reprimanded him. "Mr. Schnall, how can that be funny? I don't find any of this amusing. I really don't," she said when he laughed while the A.C.S. lawyer was reporting the "Dani's mom hit me" incident. A few pages later, this colloquy appears in the trial transcript:

> Honorable Justice Tally: Mr. Schnall, I don't know how you can make a conclusion. Have you seen your client yet?
> Mr. Schnall: No. But, I'm —
> Honorable Justice Tally: So how do you make conclusions before you've even seen your client or have any firsthand knowledge of what occurred?
> Mr. Schnall: Well —
> Honorable Justice Tally: How is that possible?

But over the years Tally had evidently grown used to Schnall, possibly even become grudgingly fond of him. At the March 9th hearing, Tally read aloud from her ruling to deny Casey's motion: "Although an attorney for the child should initially approach his role in an unbiased manner, law guardians are not expected to be neutral automatons. It is entirely appropriate and expected that over time a law guardian would form an opinion about what, if any, action would be in the best interest of his client." Tally went on:

It seems obvious in a circumstance such as the incident case that the law guardian's initial neutrality has been replaced by an opinion adverse to the respondent mother based on his view of what is in Michelle's best interest. His role as law guardian, assigned to represent a child too young to make considered judgments, is to be an advocate for the best interest of the child, not the respondent mother.

She added:

Mr. Schnall and Michelle have developed a rapport over time, since this case dates back several years, thus it would work a substantial hardship on Michelle to suddenly replace her law guardian with someone brand-new who is unfamiliar with the extensive history of this case.

When, later in the hearing, Casey returned to the issue of Schnall's removal, Tally irritably responded, "What the Court is concerned here with is Michelle's best interests, not your client's best interests, Michelle's best interests. Michelle has had this attorney for probably close to four years at this point, if not more, why should the child be penalized by having to start over with a whole new attorney at this point. Yes, he has some interest in this, and yes, he has opinions about this, but I would think you would be a neutral automaton if you did not have any kind of emotion or feelings after being this long invested in this proceeding that started out as simply a visitation/custody issue." Note how Tally moves from Michelle's best interests to Schnall's. Why should *he* be penalized for having opinions and feelings? And note, too, that Tally does not repeat the word *rapport* to describe the relationship between Schnall and Michelle, but does repeat the "neutral automaton" phrase, as if to justify her own "adverse" view of the convicted murderess.

When Scaring cross-examined Schnall at the criminal trial, he repeatedly questioned him about his insistence that the October 3rd hearing before Sidney Strauss go forward, even though the lawyers for both Malakov and Borukhova pleaded for a postponement. "They didn't want to go to the hearing on the date that you scheduled it, isn't that true?" Scaring said.

Schnall agreed. "Both of the attorneys wanted to not go that day. They didn't want to go."

"But you insisted on going that day, correct?" Scaring said.

"I did."

And so the curtain rose on the tragedy of Daniel Malakov, Michelle Malakov, and Mazoltuv Borukhova.